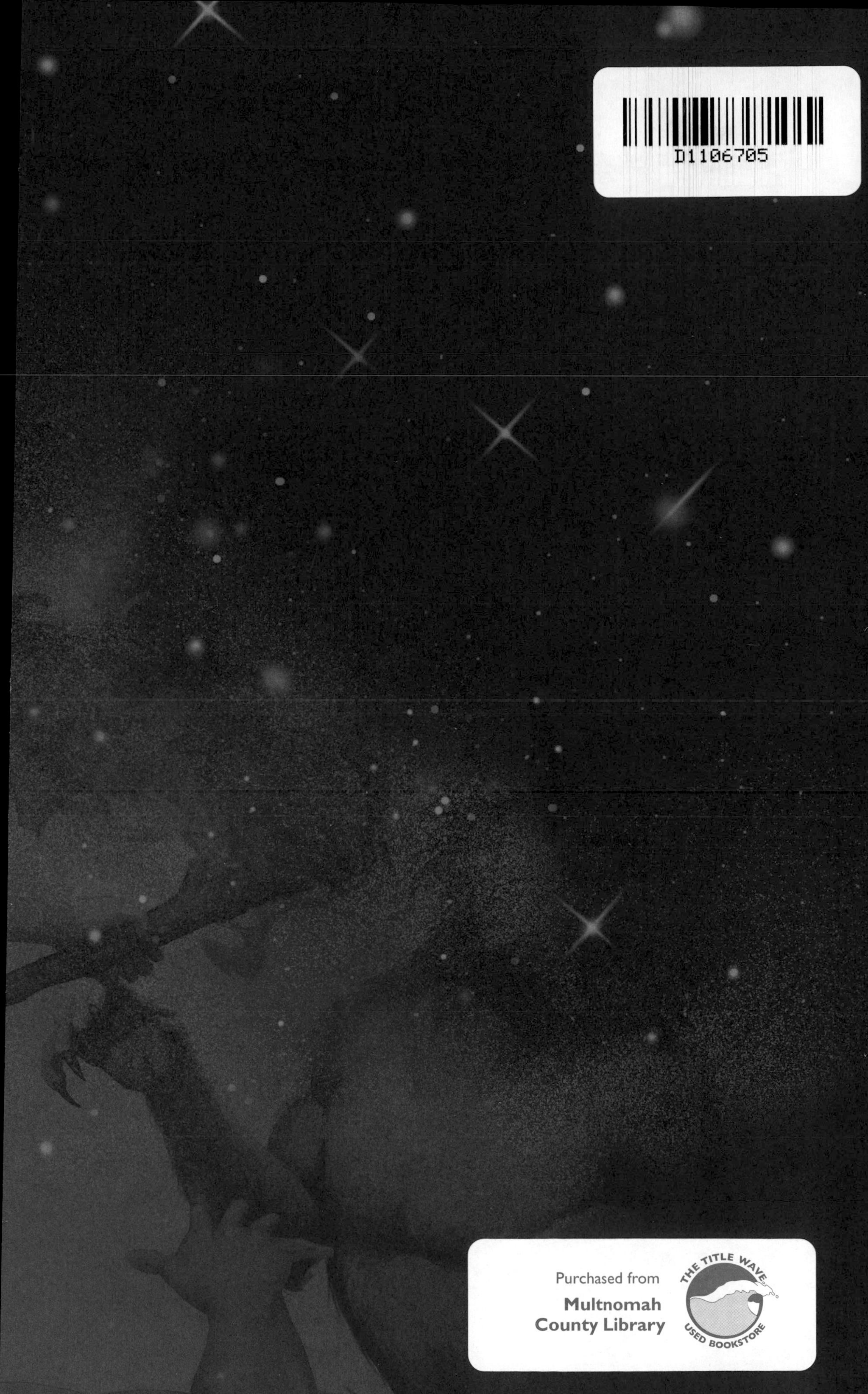

LEGENDARY COMICS

PRESENTS

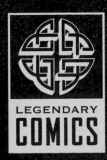

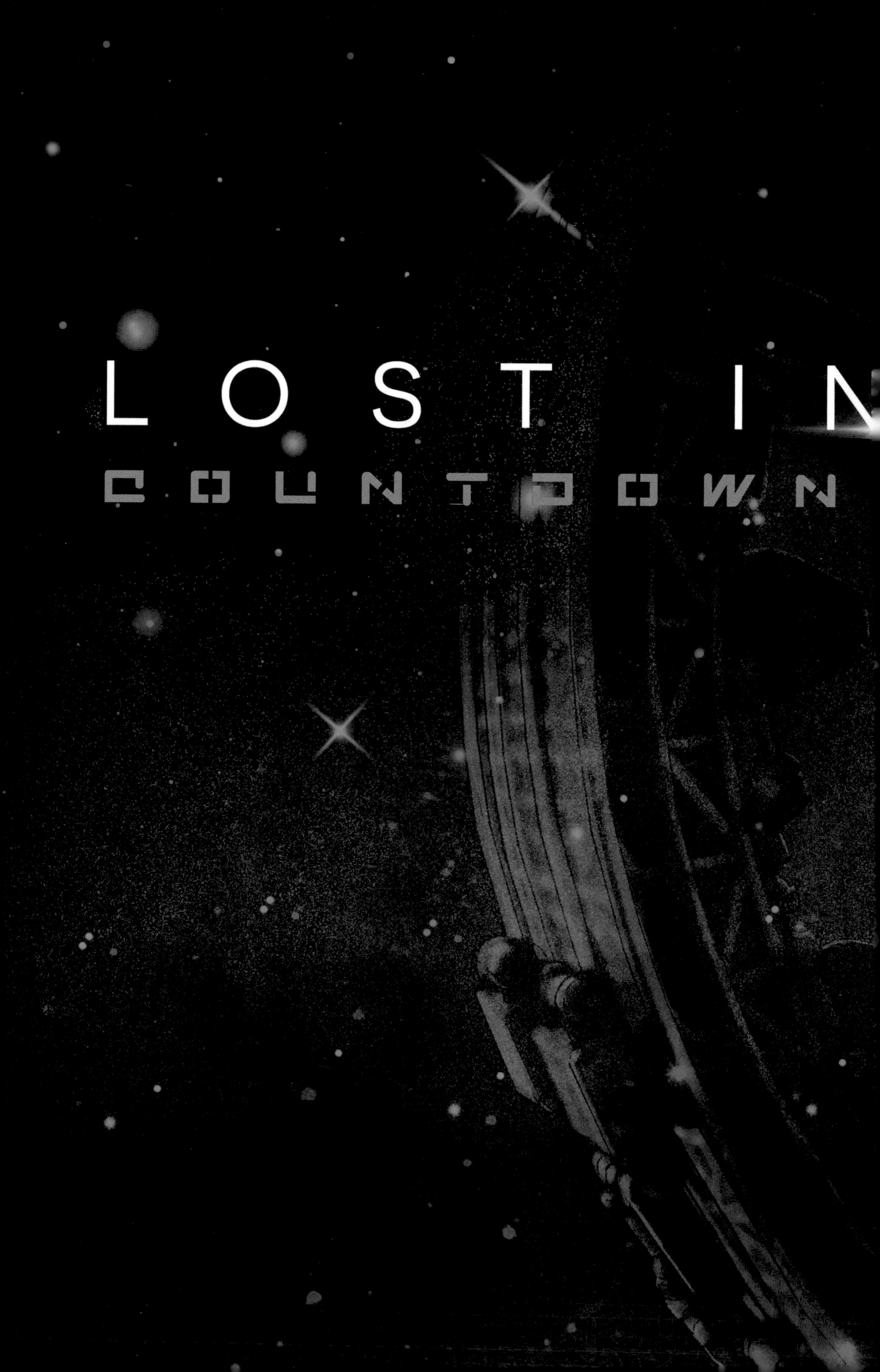
LOST IN
COUNTDOWN

SPACE TO DANGER

WRITER
BRIAN BUCCELLATO

ART
SYNCRAFT STUDIO

COVER BY
ZID

STORY CONSULTANTS
DEREK THIELGES
KEVIN BURNS
JON JASHNI

LETTERING AND DESIGN
JOHN ROSHELL, JIMMY BETANCOURT
FOREST DEMPSEY & TYLER SMITH OF **COMICRAFT**

EDITOR
ROBERT NAPTON

SPECIAL THANKS
ZACK ESTRIN
MATT SAZAMA
BURK SHARPLESS
SONIA BORRIS
MAUREEN MURPHY
OMAR KHAN
TALITHA BARKOW
THE CAST AND CREW OF LOST IN SPACE

"JUDY AND DON"

WITH THE EARTH A TOXIC MESS, PROFESSOR MAUREEN ROBINSON LED HER FAMILY – HUSBAND JOHN, DAUGHTERS PENNY AND JUDY, AND SON WILL – ON AN INCREDIBLE ADVENTURE TO A NEW COLONY ON ALPHA CENTAURI.

EN ROUTE TO THEIR NEW HOME, A STRANGE ALIEN ROBOT ATTACKS THE RESOLUTE, CAUSING MANY COLONISTS TO ABANDON SHIP.

THE ROBINSONS TAKE THE ESCAPE CRAFT JUPITER 2 AND CRASH-LAND ON AN UNKNOWN ALIEN PLANET. WITH THE SHIP DAMAGED IN A HOSTILE ENVIRONMENT, THE FAMILY STRUGGLES TO SURVIVE.

WHILE ON A MISSION TO RECOVER DESPERATELY NEEDED LIQUID METHANE FUEL FROM ANOTHER CRASHED JUPITER, JUDY ROBINSON AND ANOTHER SURVIVOR, DON WEST, FORM AN UNEASY BOND...

LEGENDARY COMICS

JOSHUA GRODE
Chief Executive Officer

MARY PARENT
Vice Chairman of
Worldwide Production

NICK PEPPER
President Of Legendary
Television & Digital Studios

RONALD HOHAUSER
Chief Financial Officer

BARNABY LEGG
SVP, Creative Strategy

MIKE ROSS
EVP, Business & Legal Affairs

KRISTINA HOLLIMAN
VP, Business & Legal Affairs

DAN FEINBERG
SVP, Corporate Counsel

BAYAN LAIRD
VP, Business & Legal Affairs

LEGENDARY COMICS

ROBERT NAPTON
SVP, Publishing

NIKITA KANNEKANTI
EDITOR

JANN JONES
MANAGER, BRAND DEVELOPMENT
& PUBLISHING OPERATIONS

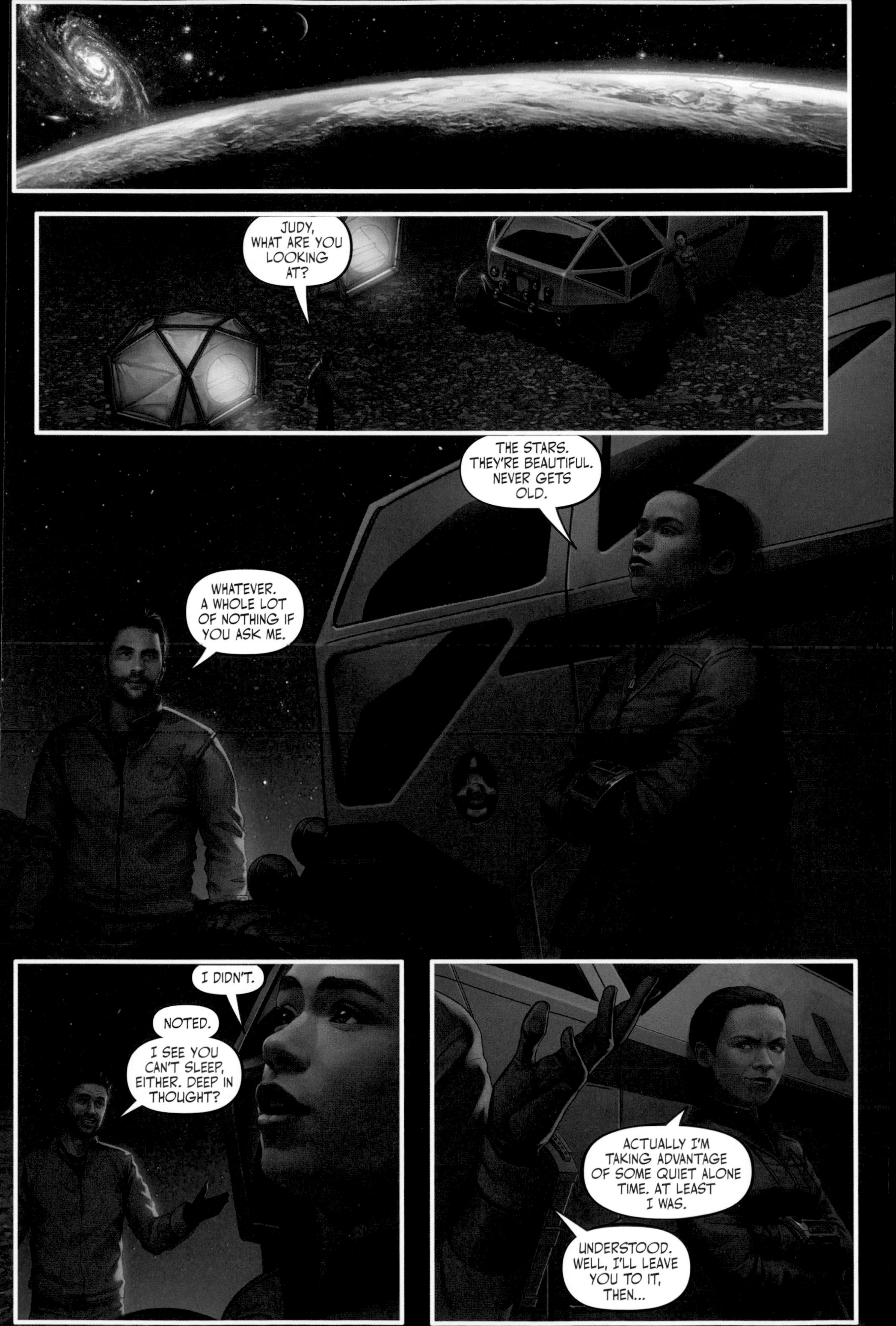
JUDY, WHAT ARE YOU LOOKING AT?
THE STARS. THEY'RE BEAUTIFUL. NEVER GETS OLD.
WHATEVER. A WHOLE LOT OF NOTHING IF YOU ASK ME.
I DIDN'T.
NOTED.
I SEE YOU CAN'T SLEEP, EITHER. DEEP IN THOUGHT?
ACTUALLY I'M TAKING ADVANTAGE OF SOME QUIET ALONE TIME. AT LEAST I WAS.
UNDERSTOOD. WELL, I'LL LEAVE YOU TO IT, THEN...

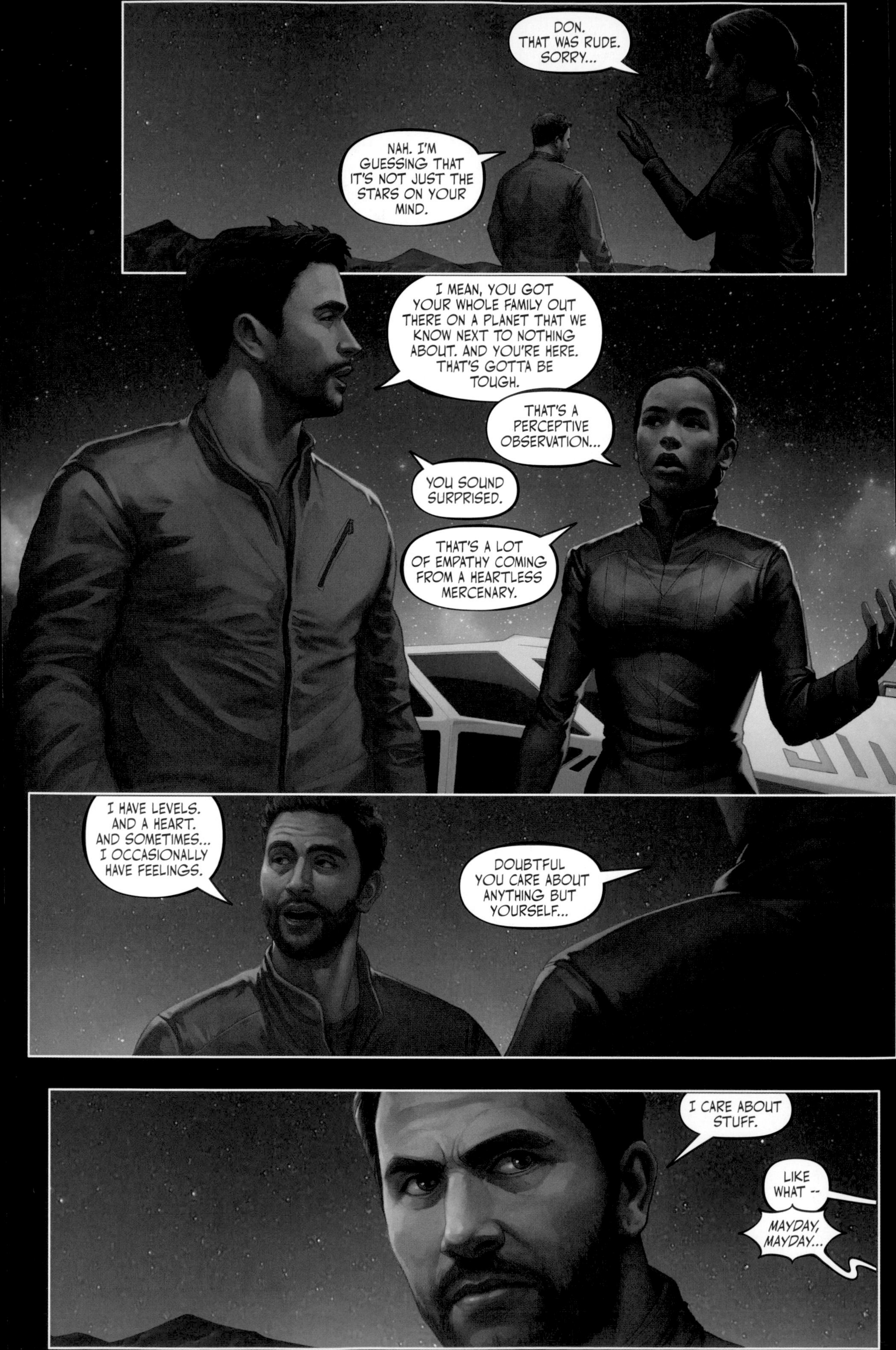
DON. THAT WAS RUDE. SORRY...
NAH. I'M GUESSING THAT IT'S NOT JUST THE STARS ON YOUR MIND.
I MEAN, YOU GOT YOUR WHOLE FAMILY OUT THERE ON A PLANET THAT WE KNOW NEXT TO NOTHING ABOUT. AND YOU'RE HERE. THAT'S GOTTA BE TOUGH.
THAT'S A PERCEPTIVE OBSERVATION...
YOU SOUND SURPRISED.
THAT'S A LOT OF EMPATHY COMING FROM A HEARTLESS MERCENARY.
I HAVE LEVELS. AND A HEART. AND SOMETIMES... I OCCASIONALLY HAVE FEELINGS.
DOUBTFUL YOU CARE ABOUT ANYTHING BUT YOURSELF...
I CARE ABOUT STUFF.
LIKE WHAT --
MAYDAY, MAYDAY...

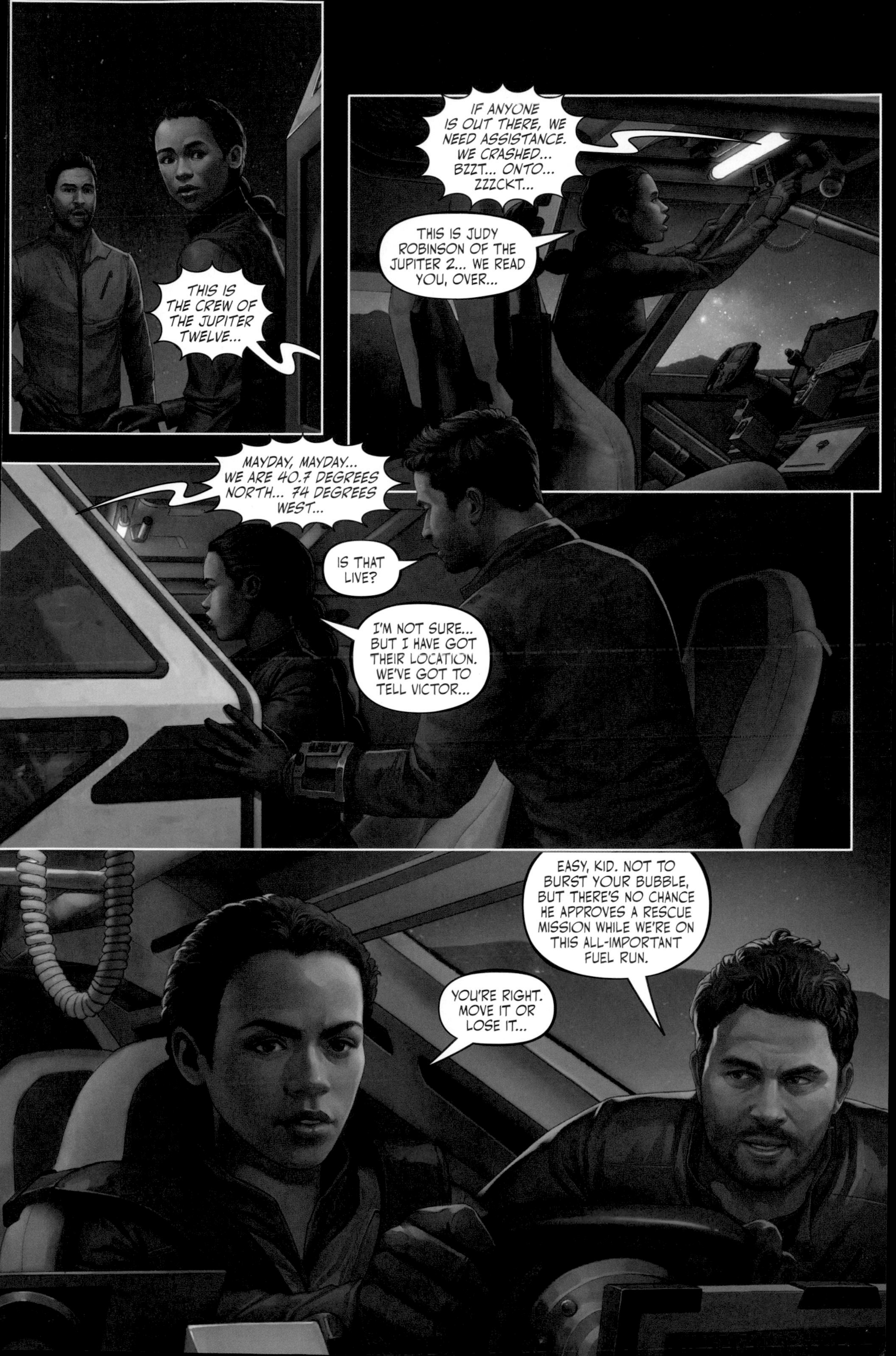
THIS IS THE CREW OF THE JUPITER TWELVE...
IF ANYONE IS OUT THERE, WE NEED ASSISTANCE. WE CRASHED... BZZT... ONTO... ZZZCKT...
THIS IS JUDY ROBINSON OF THE JUPITER 2... WE READ YOU, OVER...
MAYDAY, MAYDAY... WE ARE 40.7 DEGREES NORTH... 74 DEGREES WEST...
IS THAT LIVE?
I'M NOT SURE... BUT I HAVE GOT THEIR LOCATION. WE'VE GOT TO TELL VICTOR...
EASY, KID. NOT TO BURST YOUR BUBBLE, BUT THERE'S NO CHANCE HE APPROVES A RESCUE MISSION WHILE WE'RE ON THIS ALL-IMPORTANT FUEL RUN.
YOU'RE RIGHT. MOVE IT OR LOSE IT...

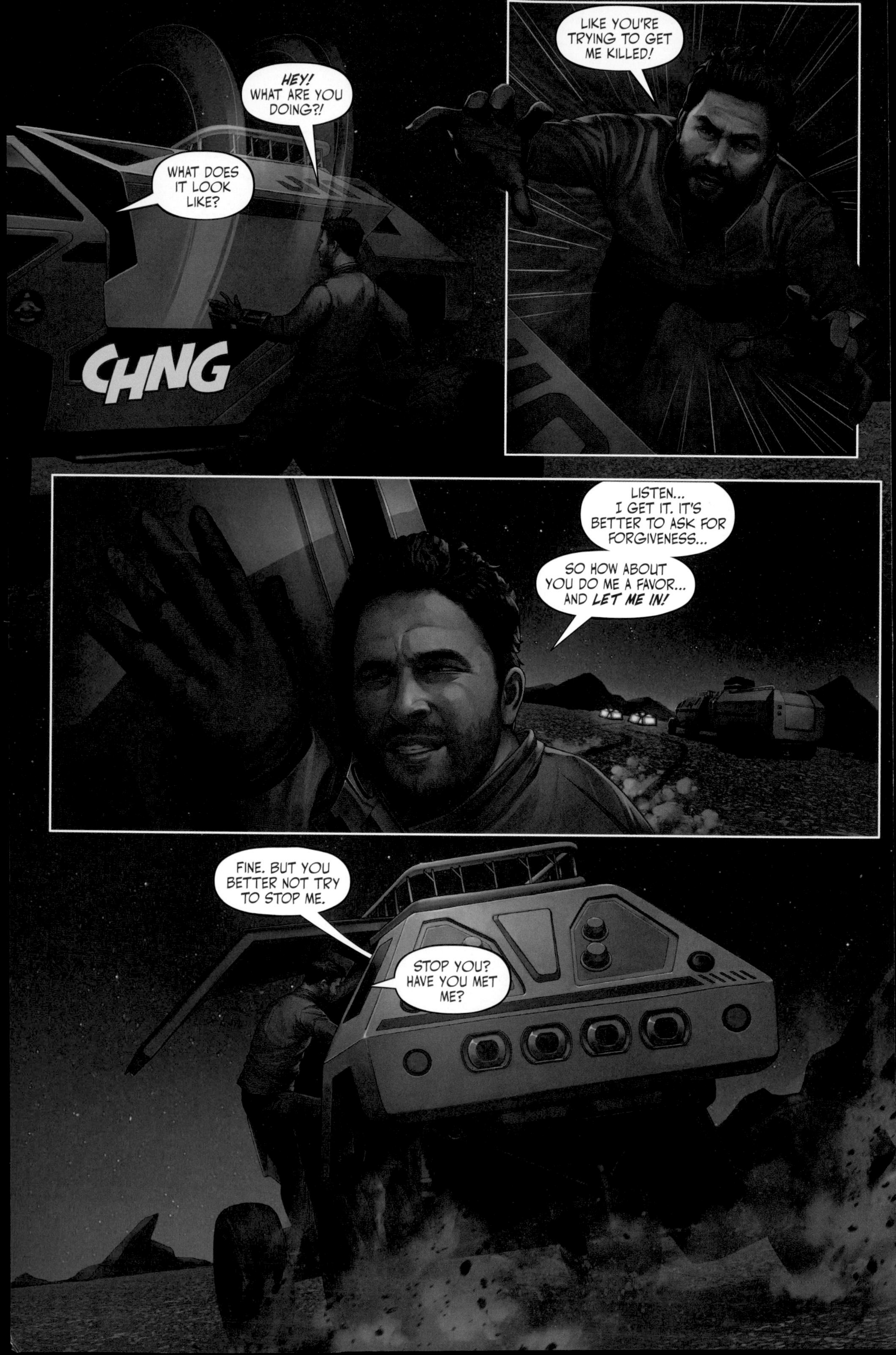
HEY! WHAT ARE YOU DOING?!
WHAT DOES IT LOOK LIKE?
CHNG
LIKE YOU'RE TRYING TO GET ME KILLED!
LISTEN... I GET IT. IT'S BETTER TO ASK FOR FORGIVENESS...
SO HOW ABOUT YOU DO ME A FAVOR... AND LET ME IN!
FINE. BUT YOU BETTER NOT TRY TO STOP ME.
STOP YOU? HAVE YOU MET ME?

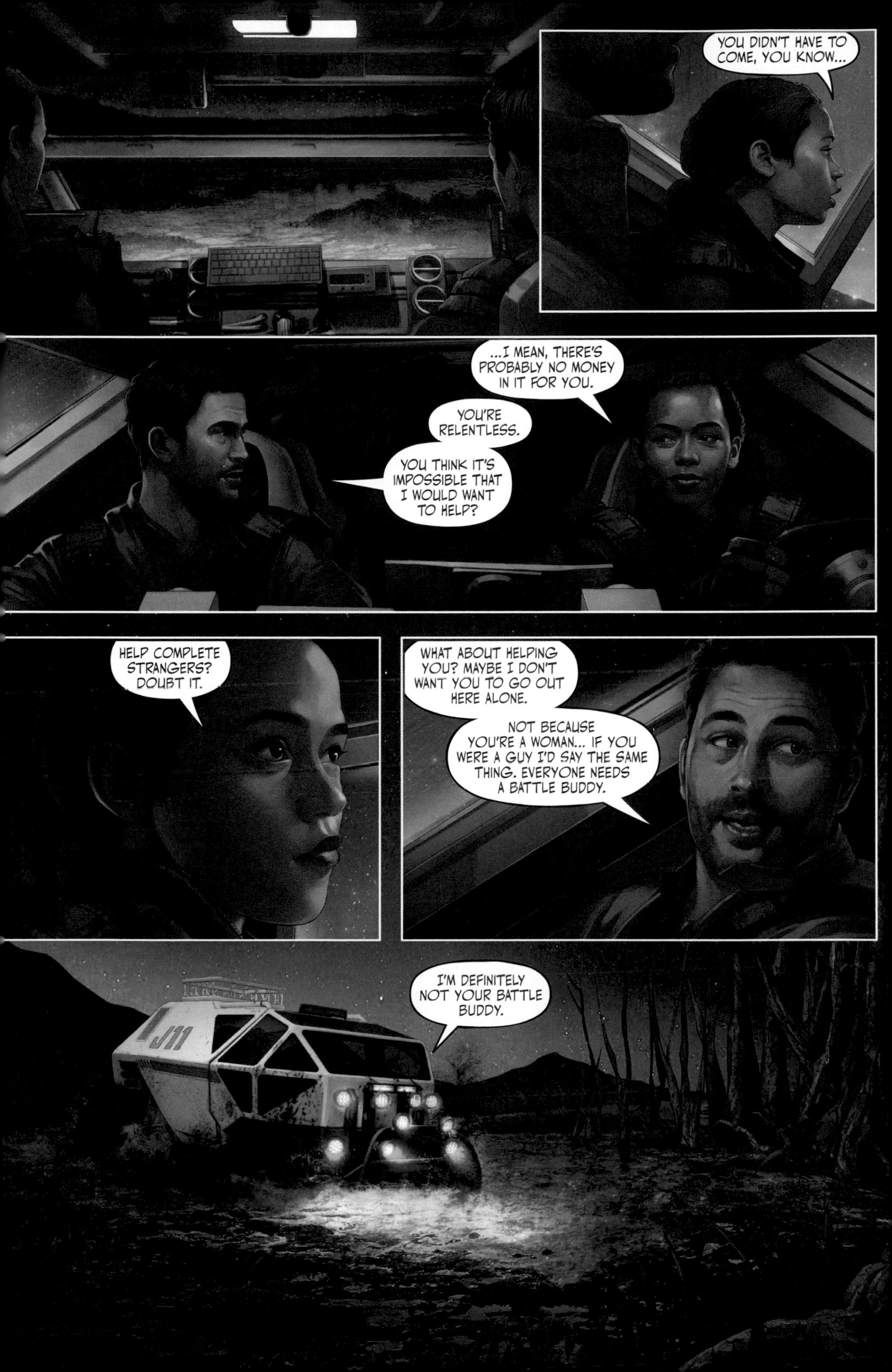
YOU DIDN'T HAVE TO COME, YOU KNOW...
...I MEAN, THERE'S PROBABLY NO MONEY IN IT FOR YOU.
YOU'RE RELENTLESS.
YOU THINK IT'S IMPOSSIBLE THAT I WOULD WANT TO HELP?
HELP COMPLETE STRANGERS? DOUBT IT.
WHAT ABOUT HELPING YOU? MAYBE I DON'T WANT YOU TO GO OUT HERE ALONE.
NOT BECAUSE YOU'RE A WOMAN... IF YOU WERE A GUY I'D SAY THE SAME THING. EVERYONE NEEDS A BATTLE BUDDY.
I'M DEFINITELY NOT YOUR BATTLE BUDDY.
J11

WELL, BUDDY... LOOKS LIKE WE'RE STUCK.

WHRRRRRRRRR

JUST STOP. OKAY... STOP.

STOP WHAT? I'M NOT THE ONE WHO GOT US STUCK...

...BUDDY.

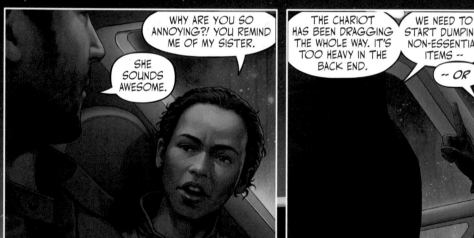

WHY ARE YOU SO ANNOYING?! YOU REMIND ME OF MY SISTER.

SHE SOUNDS AWESOME.

THE CHARIOT HAS BEEN DRAGGING THE WHOLE WAY. IT'S TOO HEAVY IN THE BACK END.

WE NEED TO START DUMPING NON-ESSENTIAL ITEMS --

-- OR

...WE DON'T DO THAT. WE DO SOMETHING ELSE INSTEAD.

THIS BUCKET HAS A WINCH, RIGHT?

YEAH...

THEN ALL WE NEED TO DO IS TO FIND SOMEPLACE TO SECURE THE TOW CABLE AND WE CAN PULL OURSELVES OUT.

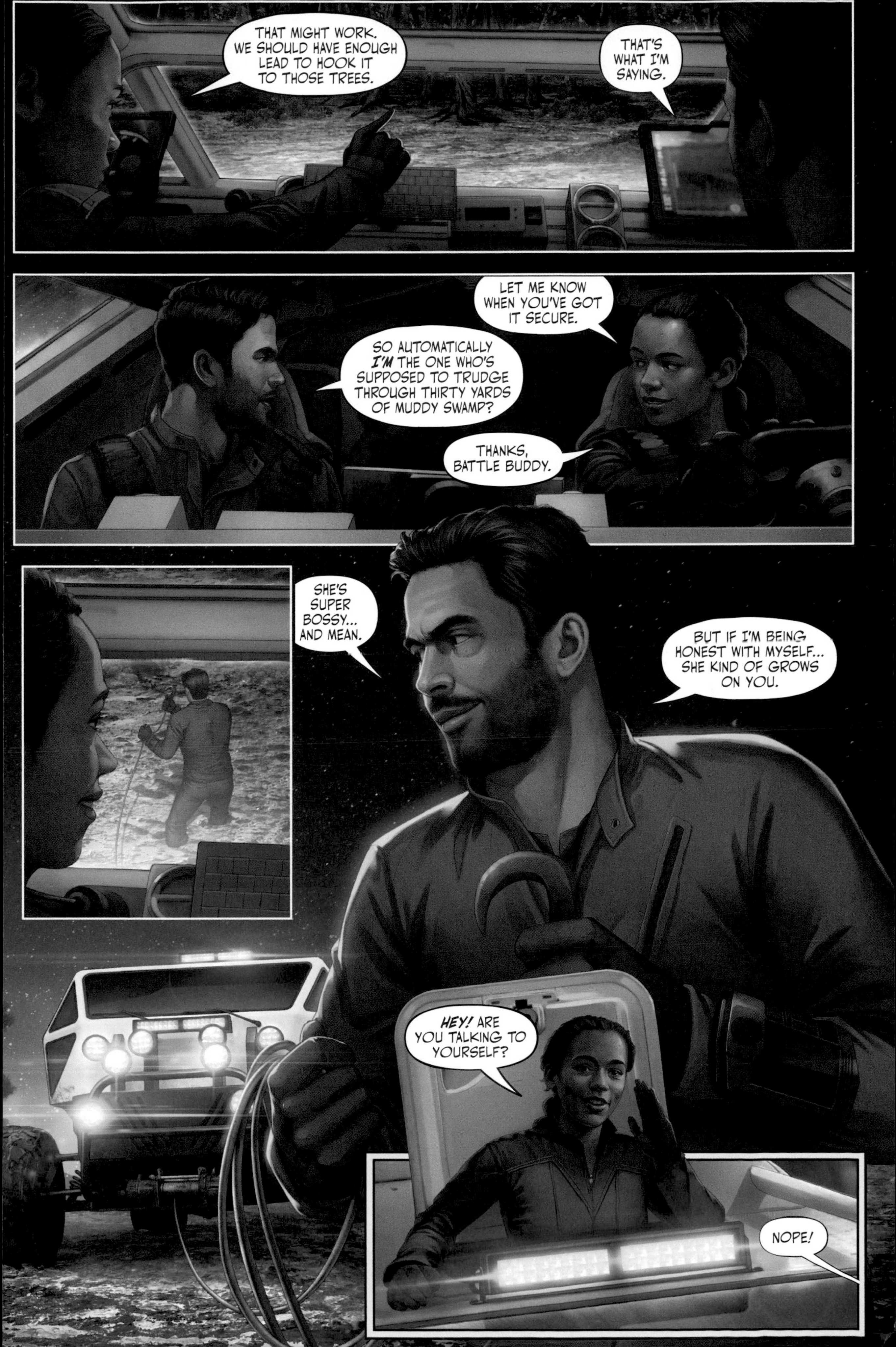
THAT MIGHT WORK. WE SHOULD HAVE ENOUGH LEAD TO HOOK IT TO THOSE TREES.
THAT'S WHAT I'M SAYING.
LET ME KNOW WHEN YOU'VE GOT IT SECURE.
SO AUTOMATICALLY *I'M* THE ONE WHO'S SUPPOSED TO TRUDGE THROUGH THIRTY YARDS OF MUDDY SWAMP?
THANKS, BATTLE BUDDY.
SHE'S SUPER BOSSY... AND MEAN.
BUT IF I'M BEING HONEST WITH MYSELF... SHE KIND OF GROWS ON YOU.
HEY! ARE YOU TALKING TO YOURSELF?
NOPE!

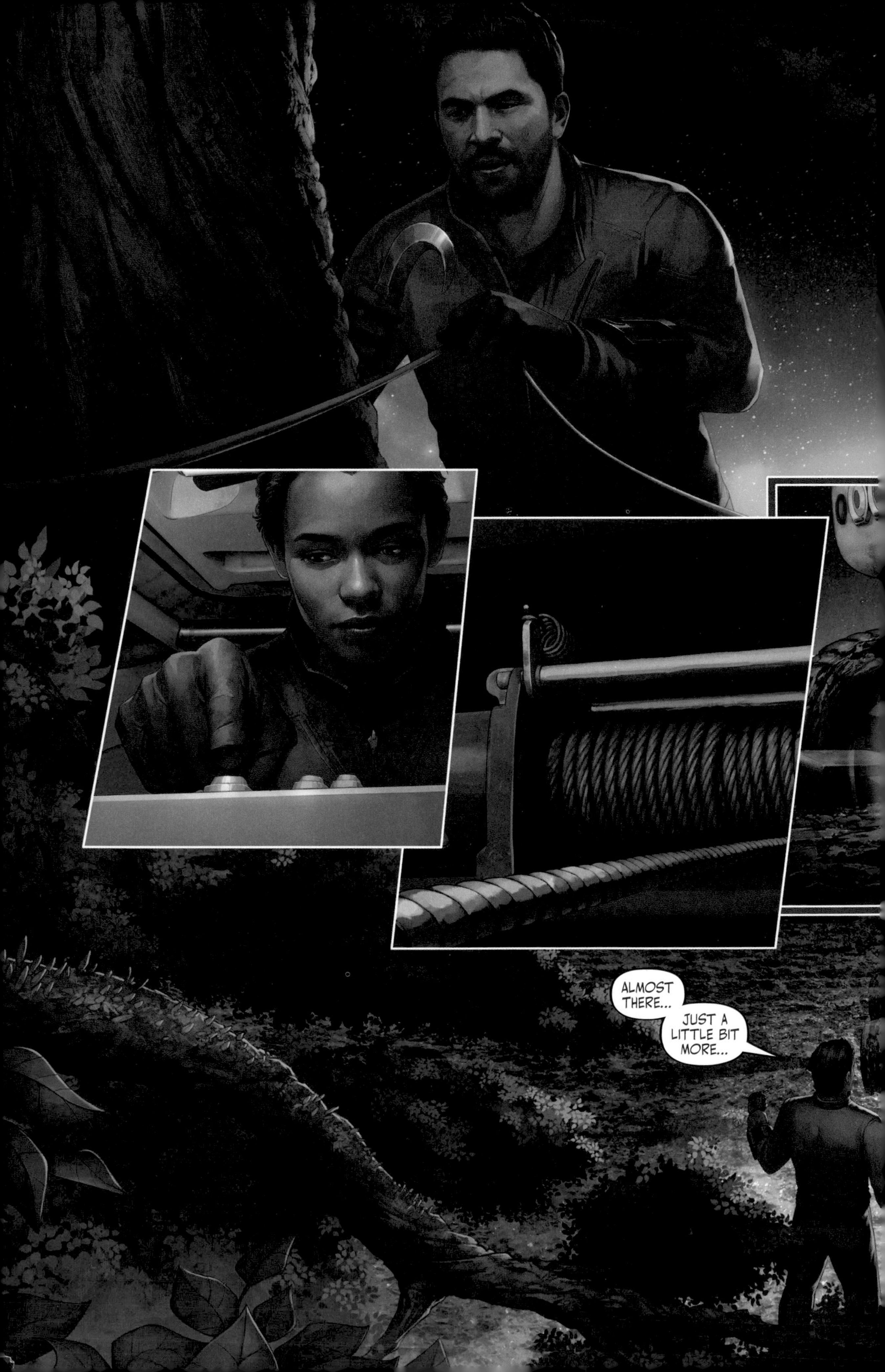
ALMOST THERE...
JUST A LITTLE BIT MORE...

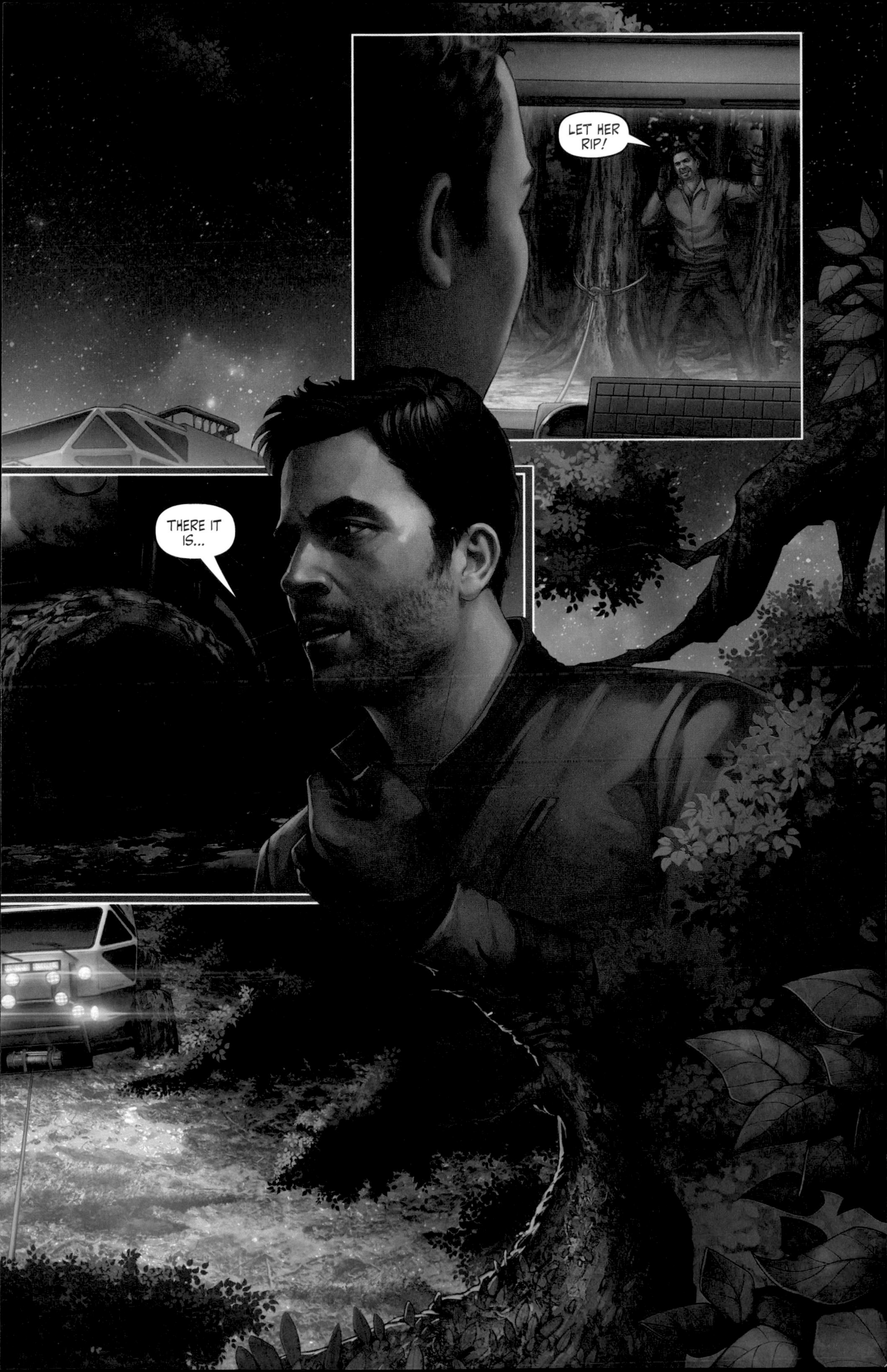
LET HER RIP!
THERE IT IS...

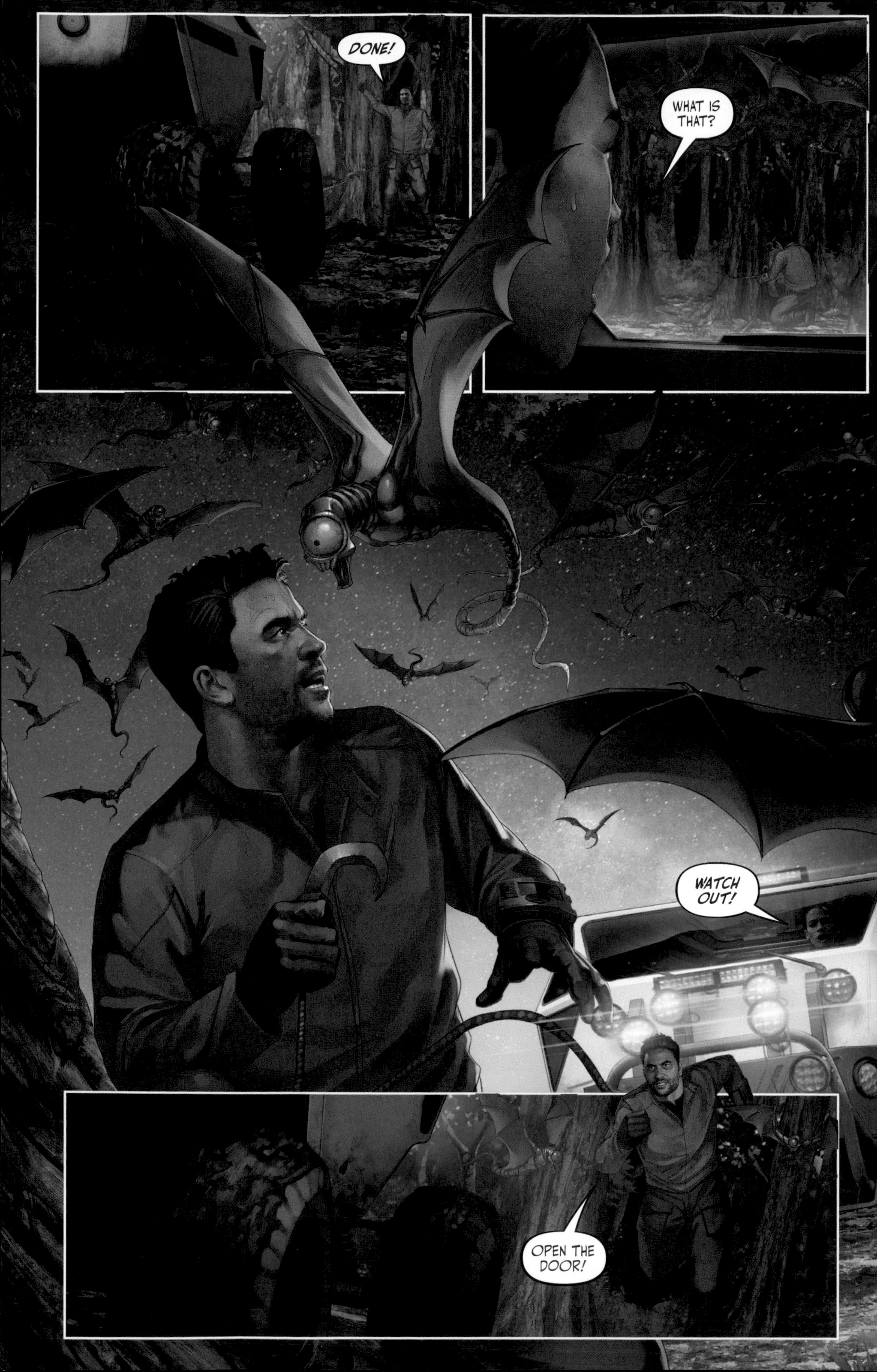
DONE!
WHAT IS THAT?
WATCH OUT!
OPEN THE DOOR!

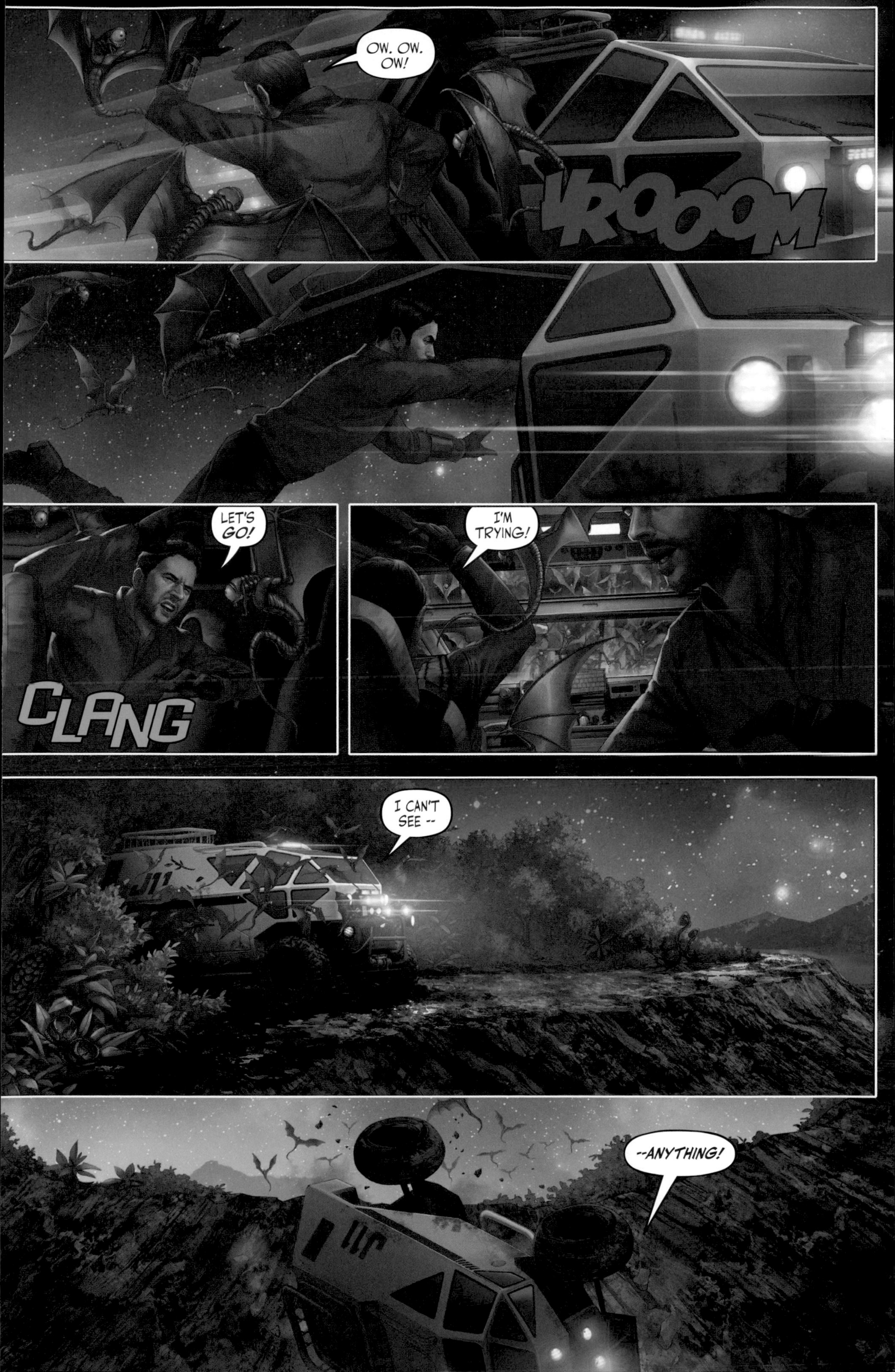
OW. OW. OW!
VROOOM
LET'S GO!
CLANG
I'M TRYING!
I CAN'T SEE --
--ANYTHING!

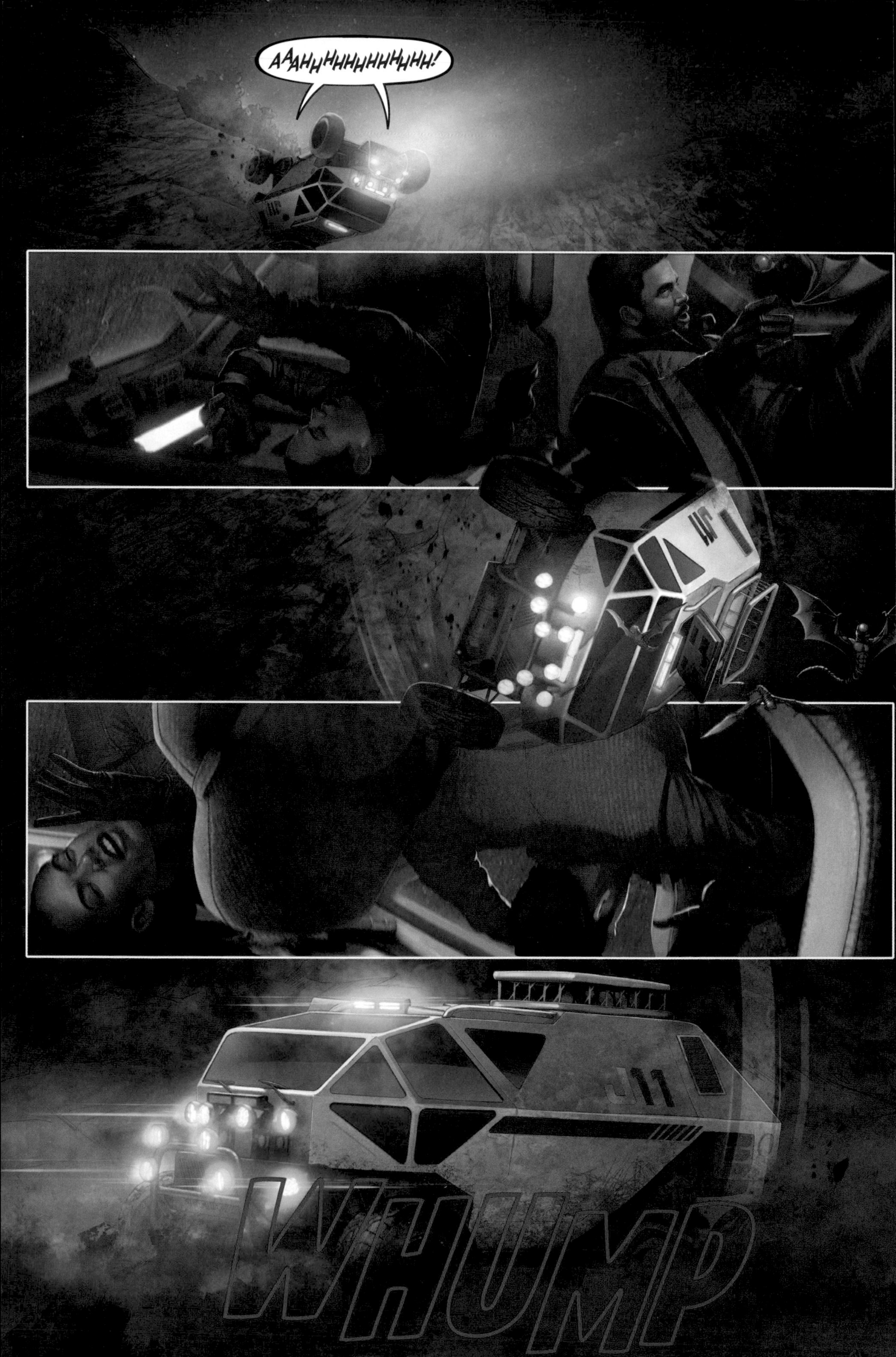
AAAHHHHHHHHHHH!
WHUMP

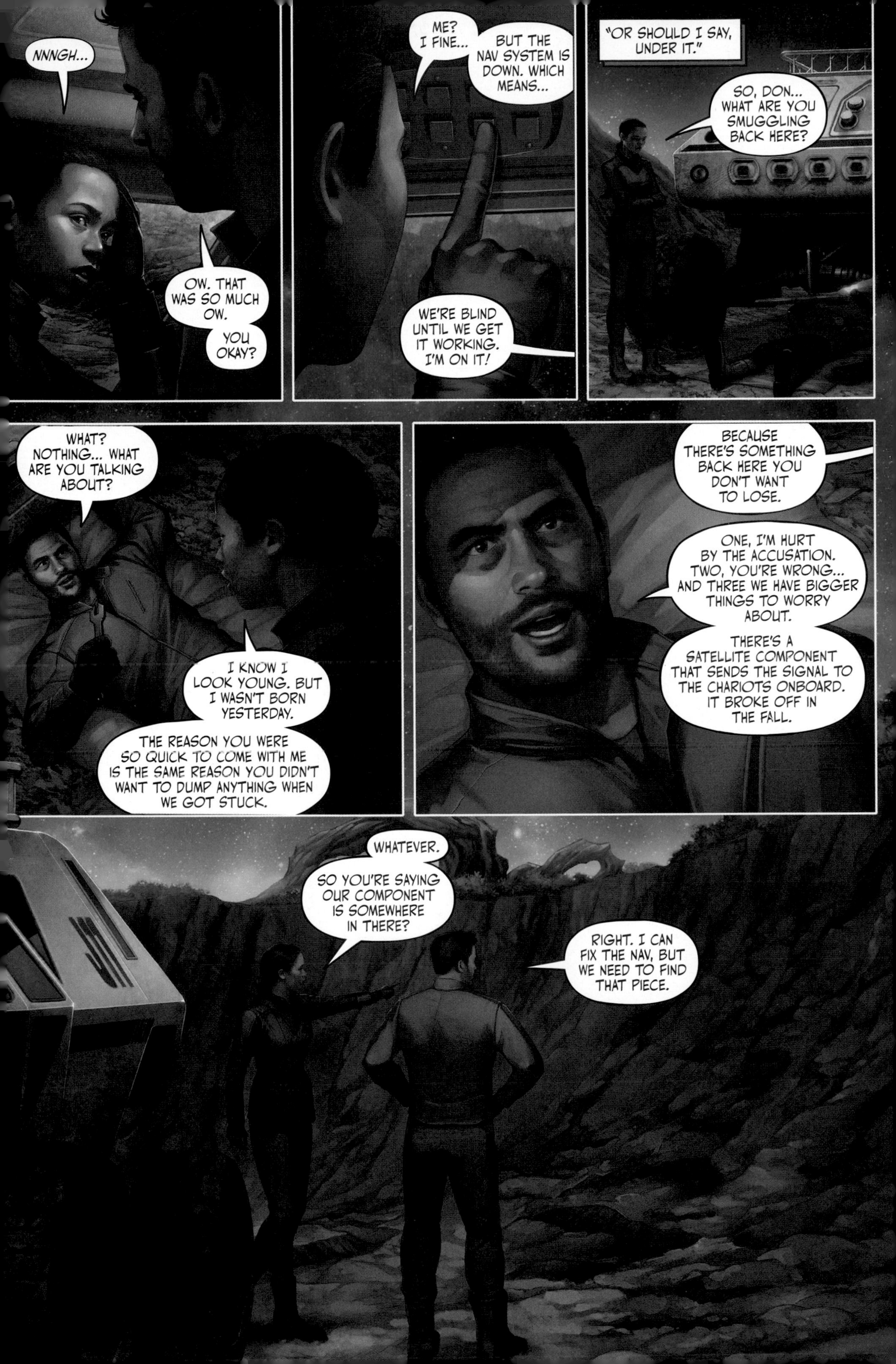
NNNGH...
OW. THAT WAS SO MUCH OW.
YOU OKAY?
ME? I FINE...
BUT THE NAV SYSTEM IS DOWN. WHICH MEANS...
WE'RE BLIND UNTIL WE GET IT WORKING. I'M ON IT!
"OR SHOULD I SAY, UNDER IT."
SO, DON... WHAT ARE YOU SMUGGLING BACK HERE?
WHAT? NOTHING... WHAT ARE YOU TALKING ABOUT?
I KNOW I LOOK YOUNG. BUT I WASN'T BORN YESTERDAY.
THE REASON YOU WERE SO QUICK TO COME WITH ME IS THE SAME REASON YOU DIDN'T WANT TO DUMP ANYTHING WHEN WE GOT STUCK.
BECAUSE THERE'S SOMETHING BACK HERE YOU DON'T WANT TO LOSE.
ONE, I'M HURT BY THE ACCUSATION. TWO, YOU'RE WRONG... AND THREE WE HAVE BIGGER THINGS TO WORRY ABOUT.
THERE'S A SATELLITE COMPONENT THAT SENDS THE SIGNAL TO THE CHARIOTS ONBOARD. IT BROKE OFF IN THE FALL.
WHATEVER.
SO YOU'RE SAYING OUR COMPONENT IS SOMEWHERE IN THERE?
RIGHT. I CAN FIX THE NAV, BUT WE NEED TO FIND THAT PIECE.

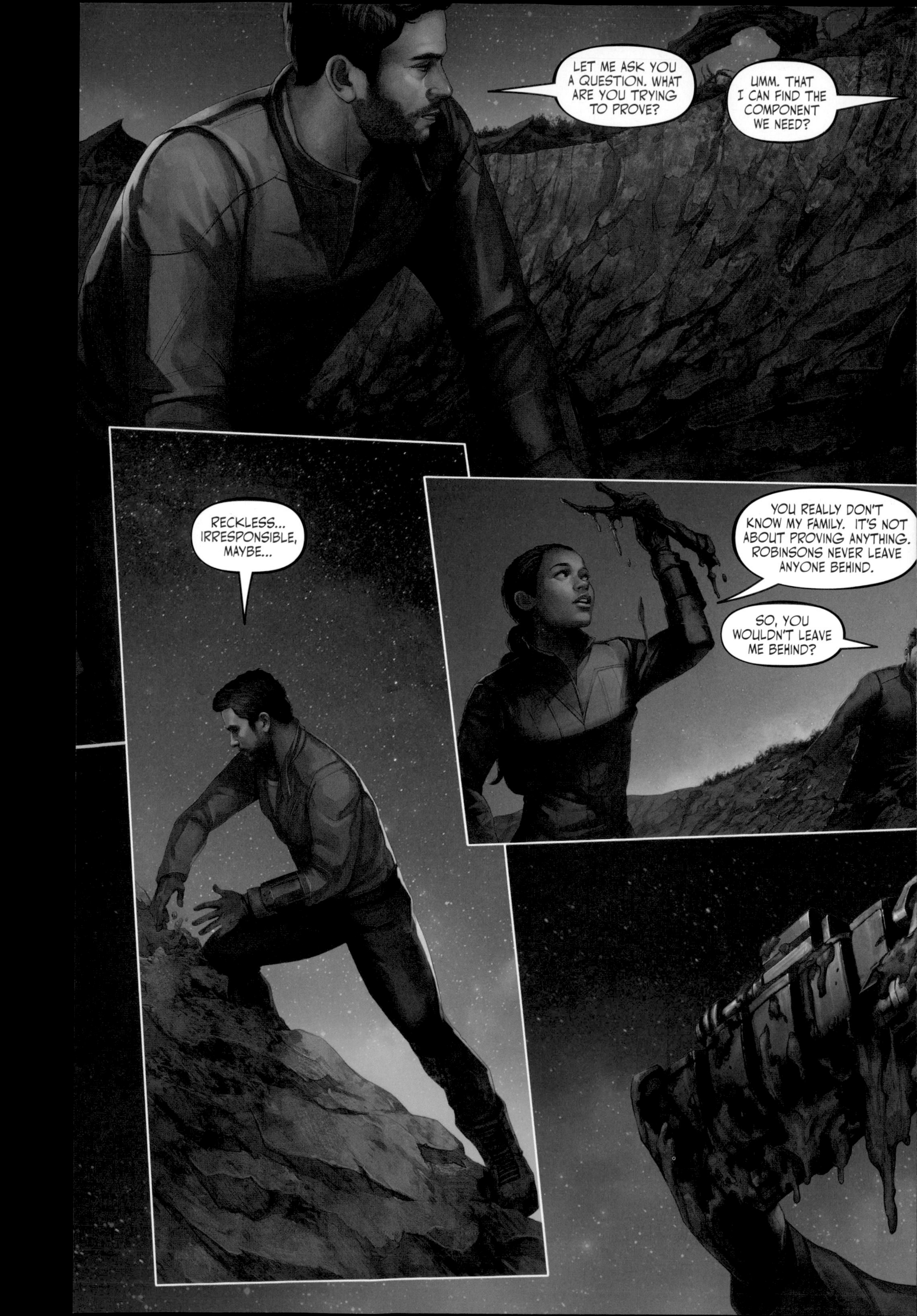

LET ME ASK YOU A QUESTION. WHAT ARE YOU TRYING TO PROVE?
UMM. THAT I CAN FIND THE COMPONENT WE NEED?
RECKLESS... IRRESPONSIBLE, MAYBE...
YOU REALLY DON'T KNOW MY FAMILY. IT'S NOT ABOUT PROVING ANYTHING. ROBINSONS NEVER LEAVE ANYONE BEHIND.
SO, YOU WOULDN'T LEAVE ME BEHIND?

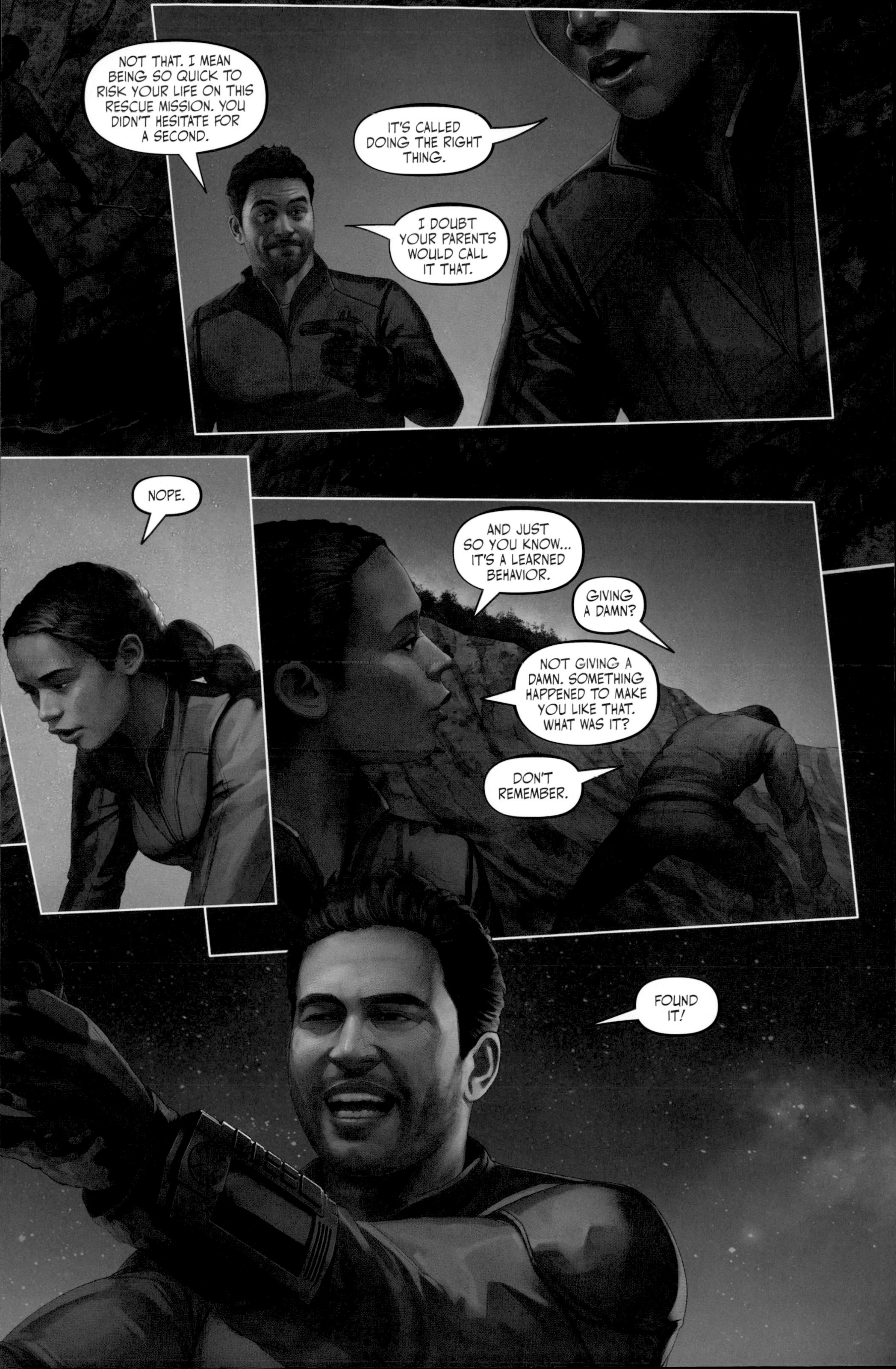
NOT THAT. I MEAN BEING SO QUICK TO RISK YOUR LIFE ON THIS RESCUE MISSION. YOU DIDN'T HESITATE FOR A SECOND.
IT'S CALLED DOING THE RIGHT THING.
I DOUBT YOUR PARENTS WOULD CALL IT THAT.
NOPE.
AND JUST SO YOU KNOW... IT'S A LEARNED BEHAVIOR.
GIVING A DAMN?
NOT GIVING A DAMN. SOMETHING HAPPENED TO MAKE YOU LIKE THAT. WHAT WAS IT?
DON'T REMEMBER.
FOUND IT!

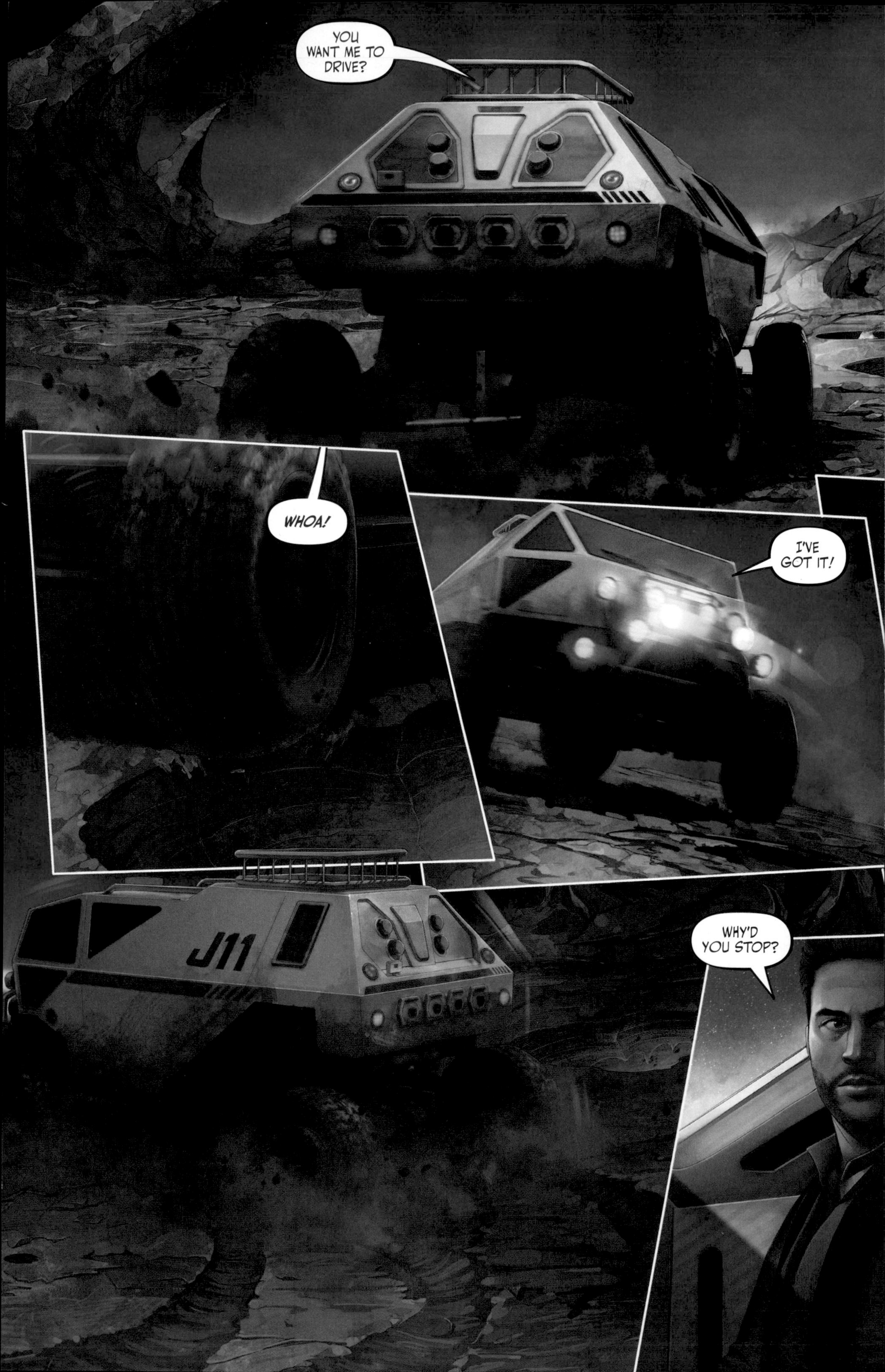
YOU WANT ME TO DRIVE?
WHOA!
I'VE GOT IT!
J11
WHY'D YOU STOP?

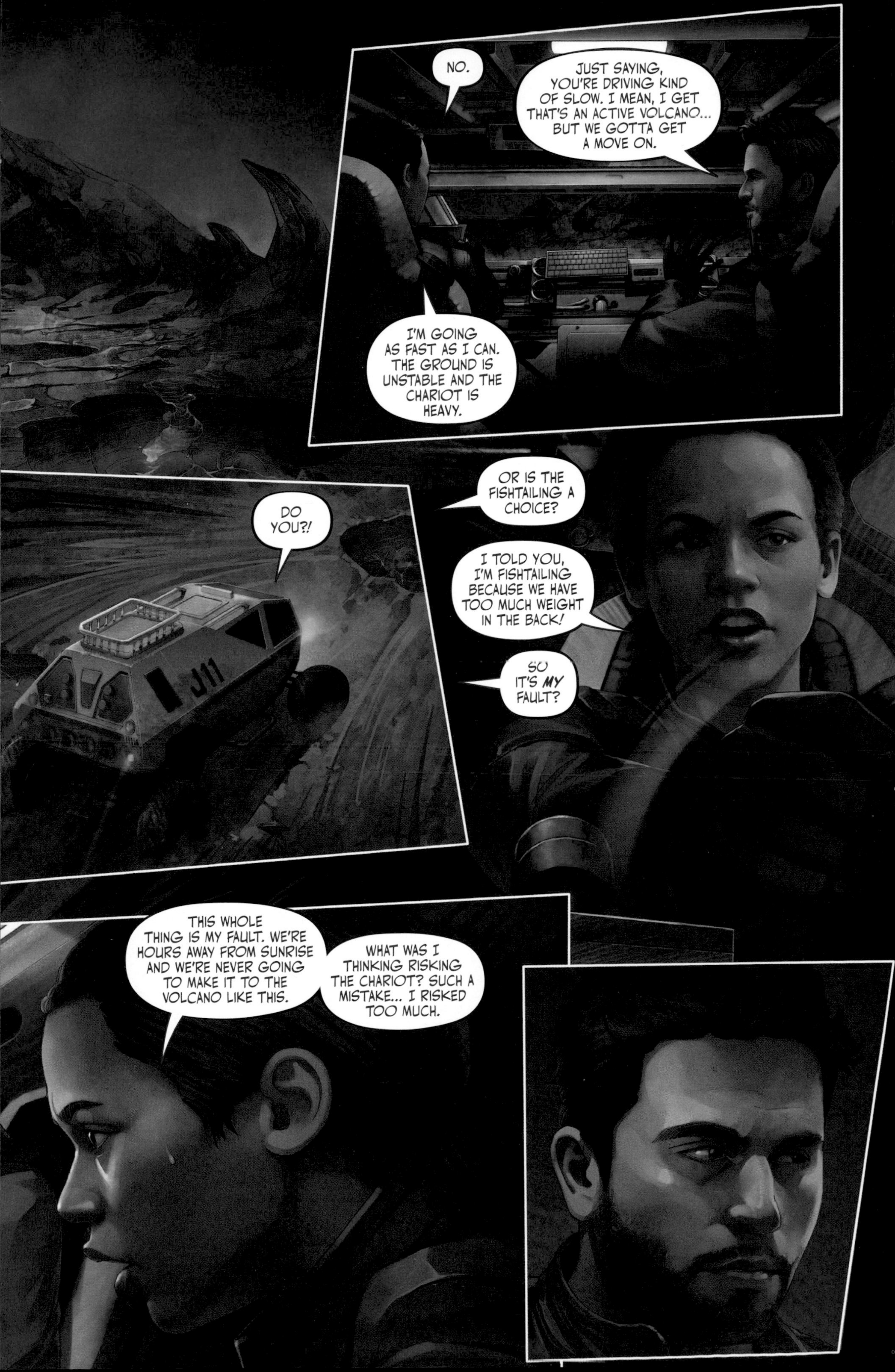
JUST SAYING, YOU'RE DRIVING KIND OF SLOW. I MEAN, I GET THAT'S AN ACTIVE VOLCANO... BUT WE GOTTA GET A MOVE ON.
NO.
I'M GOING AS FAST AS I CAN. THE GROUND IS UNSTABLE AND THE CHARIOT IS HEAVY.
DO YOU?!
OR IS THE FISHTAILING A CHOICE?
I TOLD YOU, I'M FISHTAILING BECAUSE WE HAVE TOO MUCH WEIGHT IN THE BACK!
SO IT'S *MY* FAULT?
J11
THIS WHOLE THING IS MY FAULT. WE'RE HOURS AWAY FROM SUNRISE AND WE'RE NEVER GOING TO MAKE IT TO THE VOLCANO LIKE THIS.
WHAT WAS I THINKING RISKING THE CHARIOT? SUCH A MISTAKE... I RISKED TOO MUCH.

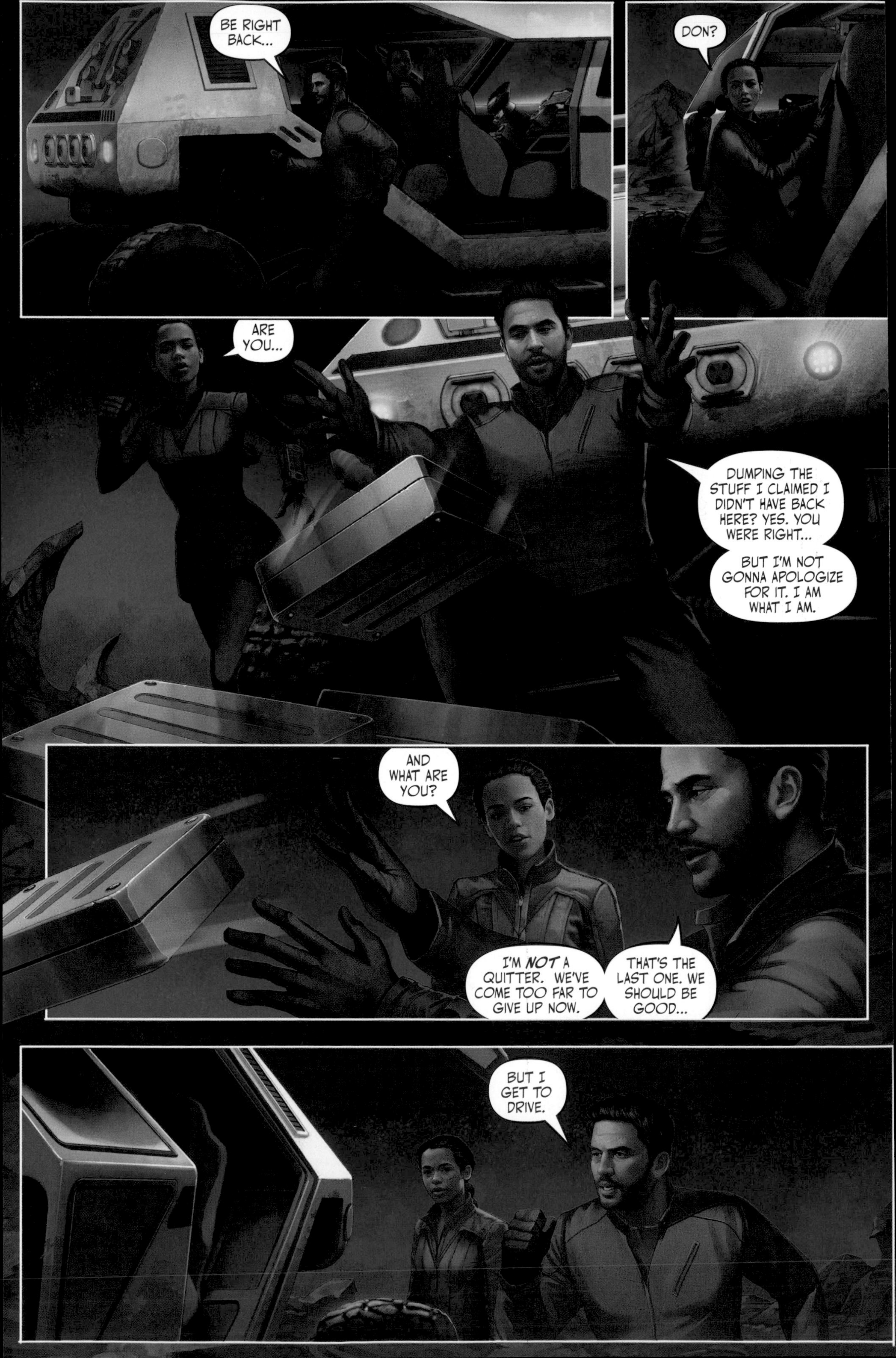
BE RIGHT BACK...
DON?
ARE YOU...
DUMPING THE STUFF I CLAIMED I DIDN'T HAVE BACK HERE? YES. YOU WERE RIGHT...
BUT I'M NOT GONNA APOLOGIZE FOR IT. I AM WHAT I AM.
AND WHAT ARE YOU?
I'M *NOT* A QUITTER. WE'VE COME TOO FAR TO GIVE UP NOW.
THAT'S THE LAST ONE. WE SHOULD BE GOOD...
BUT I GET TO DRIVE.

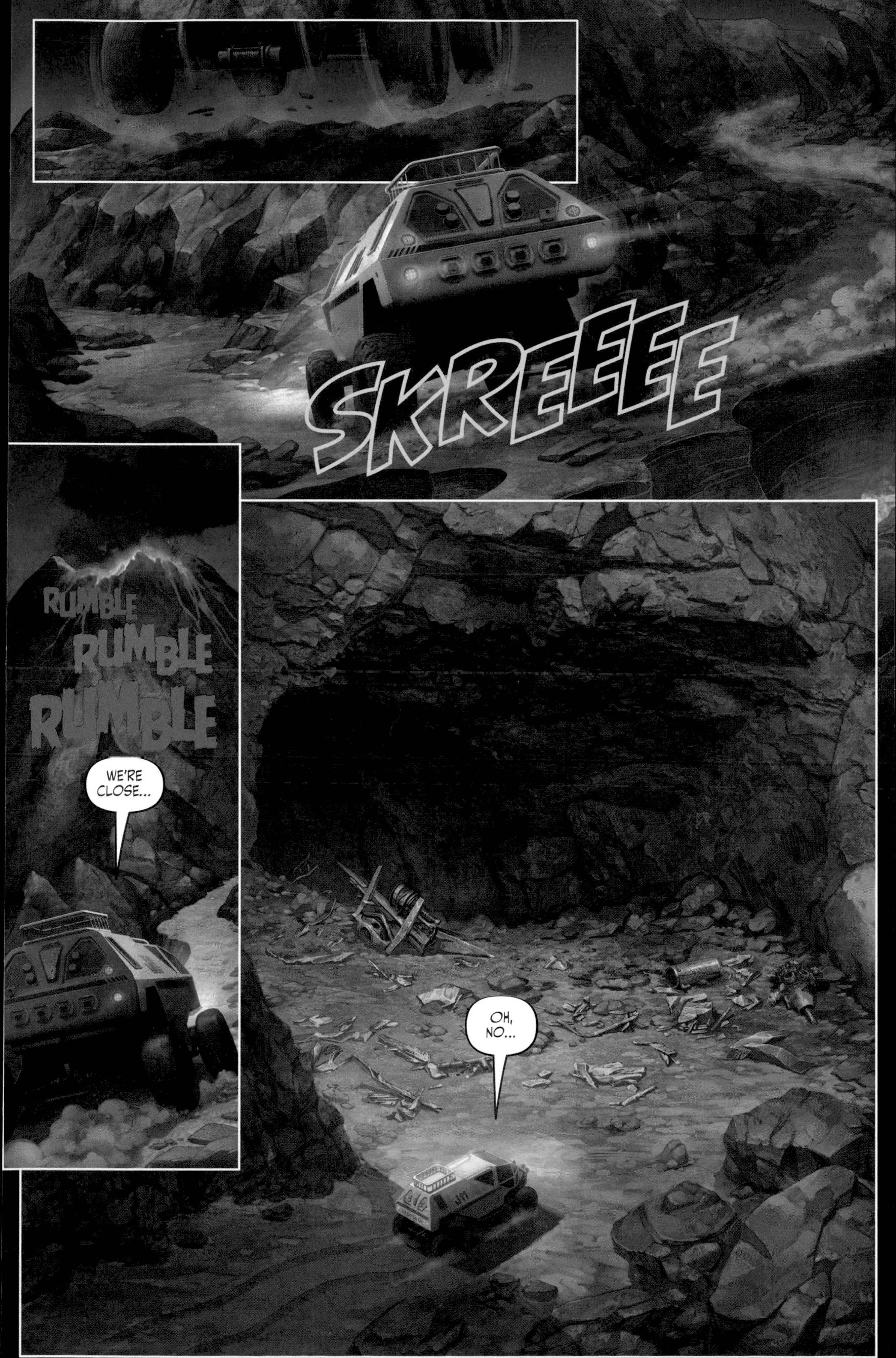
SKREEEE
RUMBLE
RUMBLE
RUMBLE
WE'RE CLOSE...
OH, NO...

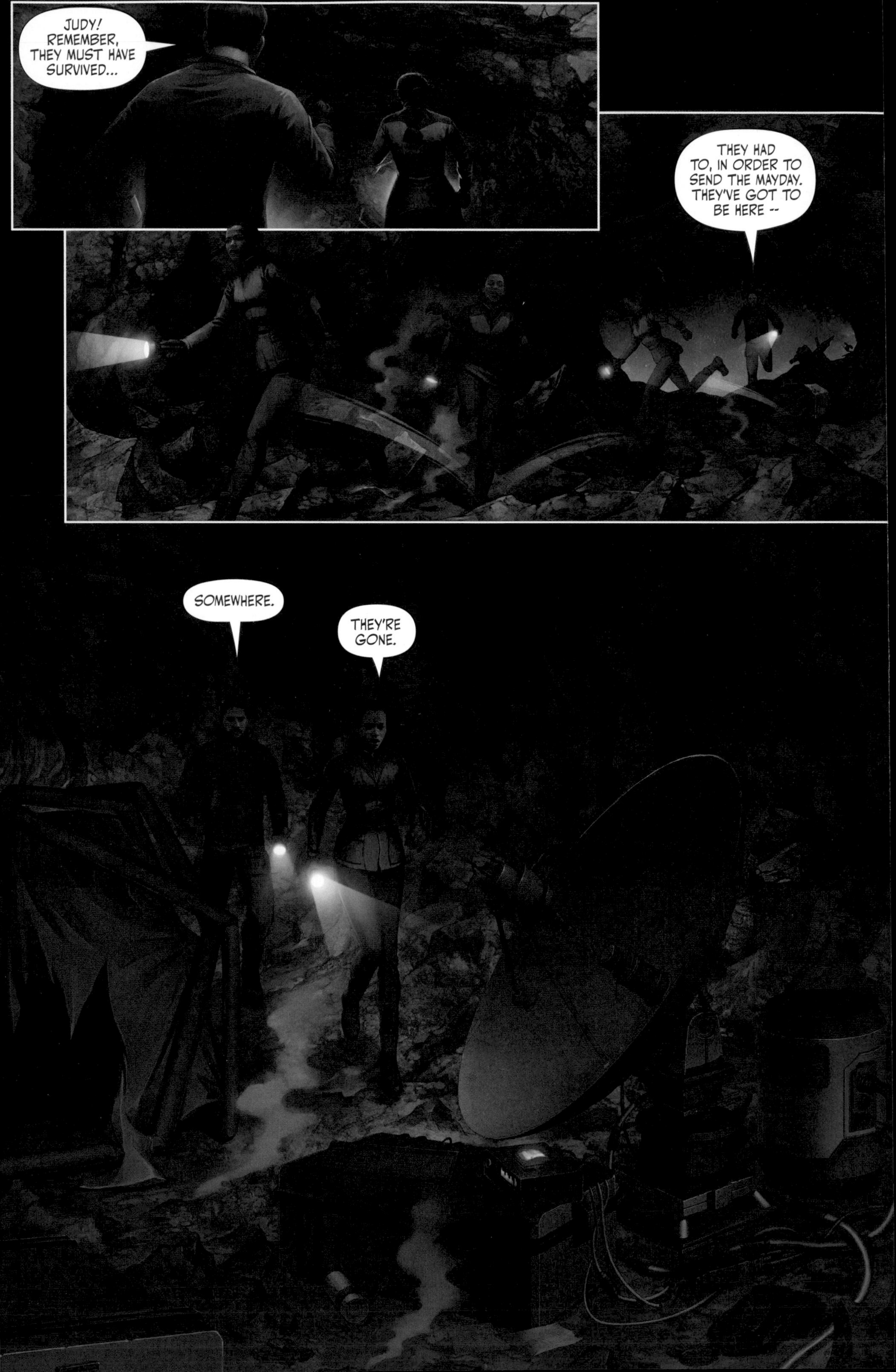
JUDY! REMEMBER, THEY MUST HAVE SURVIVED...
THEY HAD TO, IN ORDER TO SEND THE MAYDAY. THEY'VE GOT TO BE HERE --
SOMEWHERE.
THEY'RE GONE.

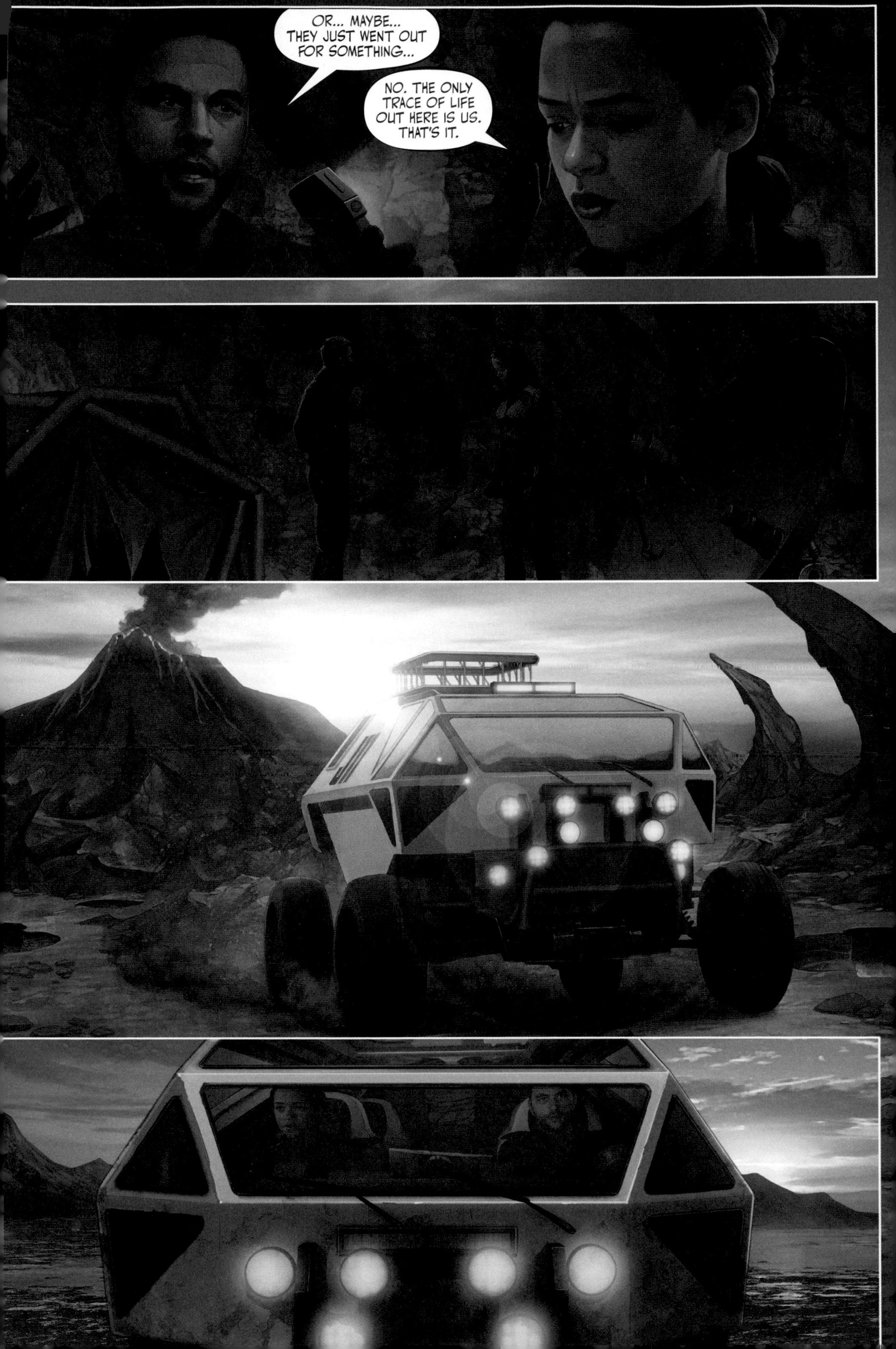
OR... MAYBE... THEY JUST WENT OUT FOR SOMETHING...
NO. THE ONLY TRACE OF LIFE OUT HERE IS US. THAT'S IT.

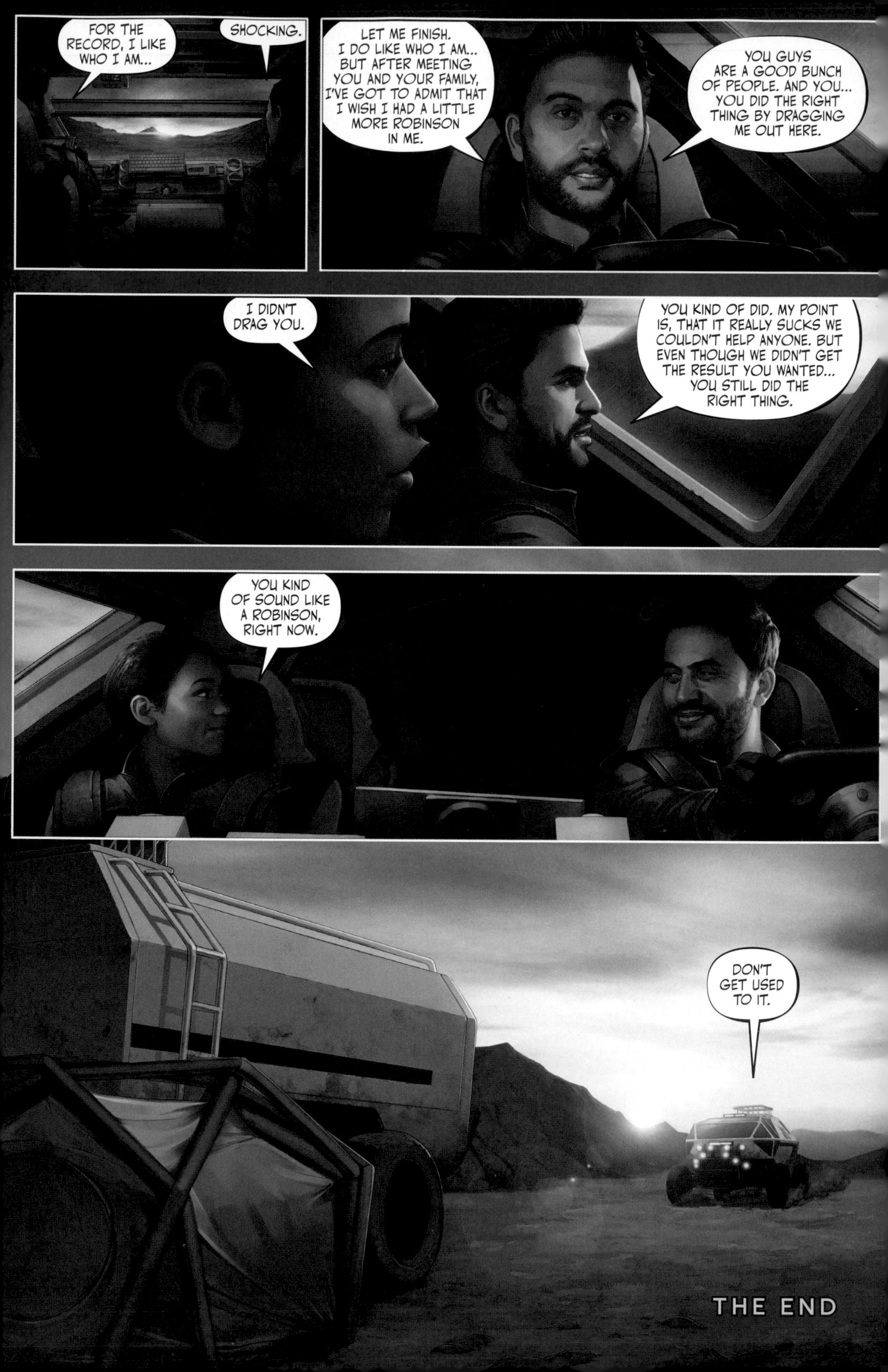
FOR THE RECORD, I LIKE WHO I AM...
SHOCKING.
LET ME FINISH. I DO LIKE WHO I AM... BUT AFTER MEETING YOU AND YOUR FAMILY, I'VE GOT TO ADMIT THAT I WISH I HAD A LITTLE MORE ROBINSON IN ME.
YOU GUYS ARE A GOOD BUNCH OF PEOPLE. AND YOU... YOU DID THE RIGHT THING BY DRAGGING ME OUT HERE.
I DIDN'T DRAG YOU.
YOU KIND OF DID. MY POINT IS, THAT IT REALLY SUCKS WE COULDN'T HELP ANYONE. BUT EVEN THOUGH WE DIDN'T GET THE RESULT YOU WANTED... YOU STILL DID THE RIGHT THING.
YOU KIND OF SOUND LIKE A ROBINSON, RIGHT NOW.
DON'T GET USED TO IT.
THE END

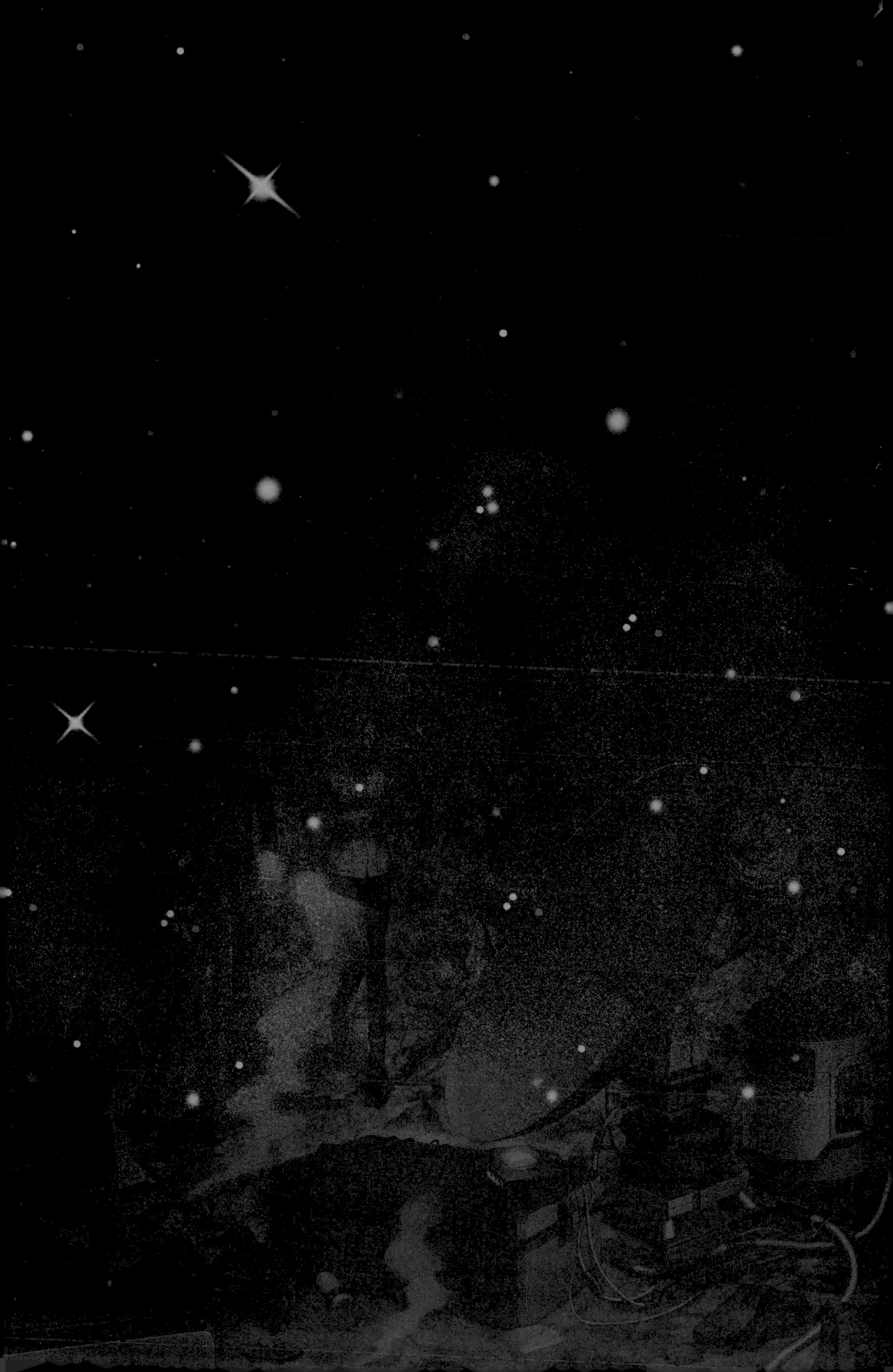

"JOHN AND MAUREEN"

AFTER THEIR CHARIOT CRASHES INTO A LAKE
OF TAR, JOHN AND MAUREEN SINK BELOW THE
SURFACE AND NEARLY SUFFOCATE TO DEATH.

AFTER A HARROWING ESCAPE FROM THE TAR, THE
ELDER ROBINSONS MAKE THEIR WAY BACK ON
FOOT ACROSS THE UNKNOWN ALIEN WORLD...

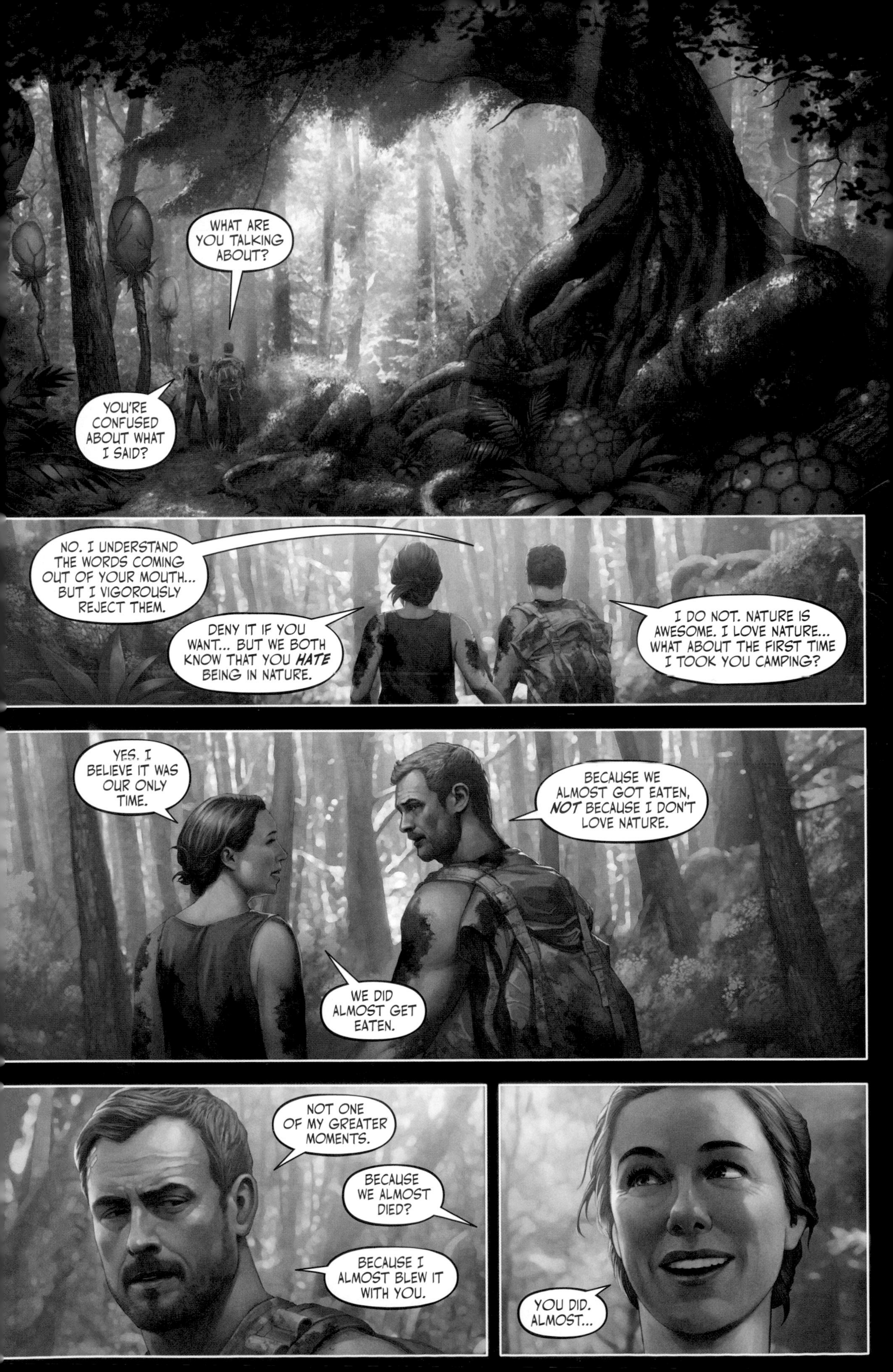
WHAT ARE YOU TALKING ABOUT?
YOU'RE CONFUSED ABOUT WHAT I SAID?
NO. I UNDERSTAND THE WORDS COMING OUT OF YOUR MOUTH... BUT I VIGOROUSLY REJECT THEM.
DENY IT IF YOU WANT... BUT WE BOTH KNOW THAT YOU HATE BEING IN NATURE.
I DO NOT. NATURE IS AWESOME. I LOVE NATURE... WHAT ABOUT THE FIRST TIME I TOOK YOU CAMPING?
YES. I BELIEVE IT WAS OUR ONLY TIME.
BECAUSE WE ALMOST GOT EATEN, NOT BECAUSE I DON'T LOVE NATURE.
WE DID ALMOST GET EATEN.
NOT ONE OF MY GREATER MOMENTS.
BECAUSE WE ALMOST DIED?
BECAUSE I ALMOST BLEW IT WITH YOU.
YOU DID. ALMOST...

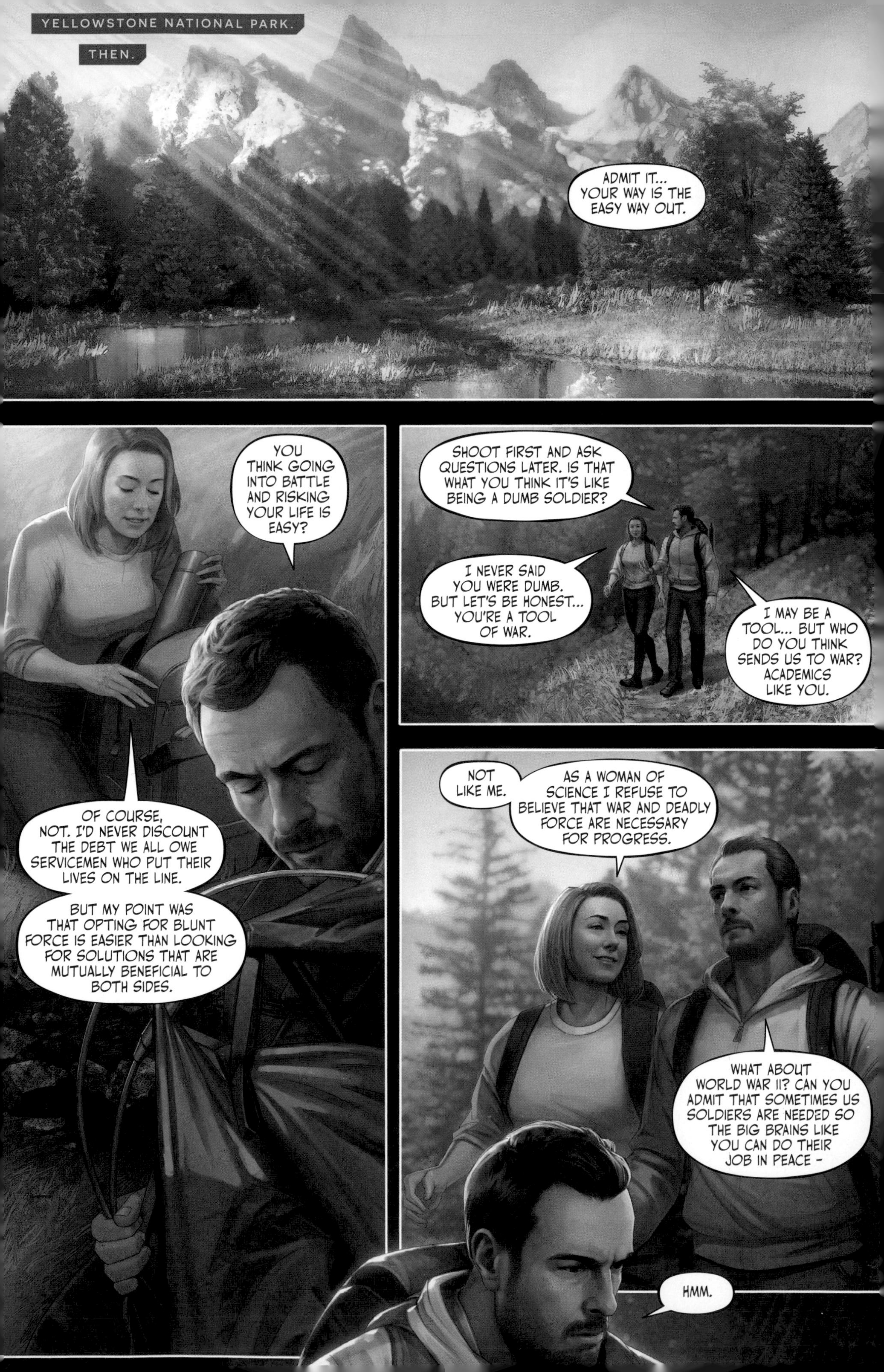
YELLOWSTONE NATIONAL PARK.
THEN.
ADMIT IT... YOUR WAY IS THE EASY WAY OUT.
YOU THINK GOING INTO BATTLE AND RISKING YOUR LIFE IS EASY?
OF COURSE, NOT. I'D NEVER DISCOUNT THE DEBT WE ALL OWE SERVICEMEN WHO PUT THEIR LIVES ON THE LINE.
BUT MY POINT WAS THAT OPTING FOR BLUNT FORCE IS EASIER THAN LOOKING FOR SOLUTIONS THAT ARE MUTUALLY BENEFICIAL TO BOTH SIDES.
SHOOT FIRST AND ASK QUESTIONS LATER. IS THAT WHAT YOU THINK IT'S LIKE BEING A DUMB SOLDIER?
I NEVER SAID YOU WERE DUMB. BUT LET'S BE HONEST... YOU'RE A TOOL OF WAR.
I MAY BE A TOOL... BUT WHO DO YOU THINK SENDS US TO WAR? ACADEMICS LIKE YOU.
NOT LIKE ME.
AS A WOMAN OF SCIENCE I REFUSE TO BELIEVE THAT WAR AND DEADLY FORCE ARE NECESSARY FOR PROGRESS.
WHAT ABOUT WORLD WAR II? CAN YOU ADMIT THAT SOMETIMES US SOLDIERS ARE NEEDED SO THE BIG BRAINS LIKE YOU CAN DO THEIR JOB IN PEACE -
HMM.

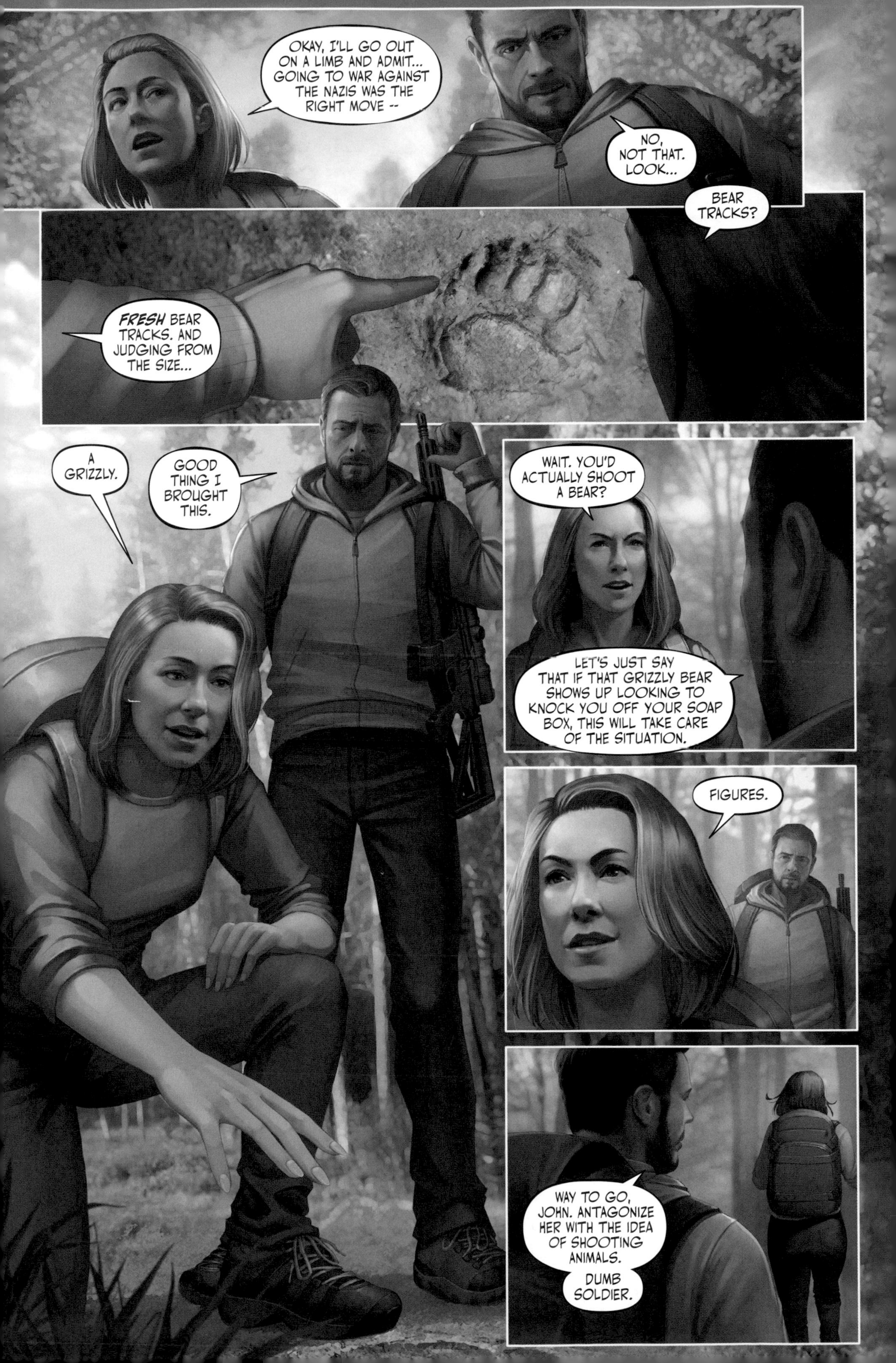
OKAY, I'LL GO OUT ON A LIMB AND ADMIT... GOING TO WAR AGAINST THE NAZIS WAS THE RIGHT MOVE --
NO, NOT THAT. LOOK...
BEAR TRACKS?
FRESH BEAR TRACKS. AND JUDGING FROM THE SIZE...
A GRIZZLY.
GOOD THING I BROUGHT THIS.
WAIT. YOU'D ACTUALLY SHOOT A BEAR?
LET'S JUST SAY THAT IF THAT GRIZZLY BEAR SHOWS UP LOOKING TO KNOCK YOU OFF YOUR SOAP BOX, THIS WILL TAKE CARE OF THE SITUATION.
FIGURES.
WAY TO GO, JOHN. ANTAGONIZE HER WITH THE IDEA OF SHOOTING ANIMALS.
DUMB SOLDIER.

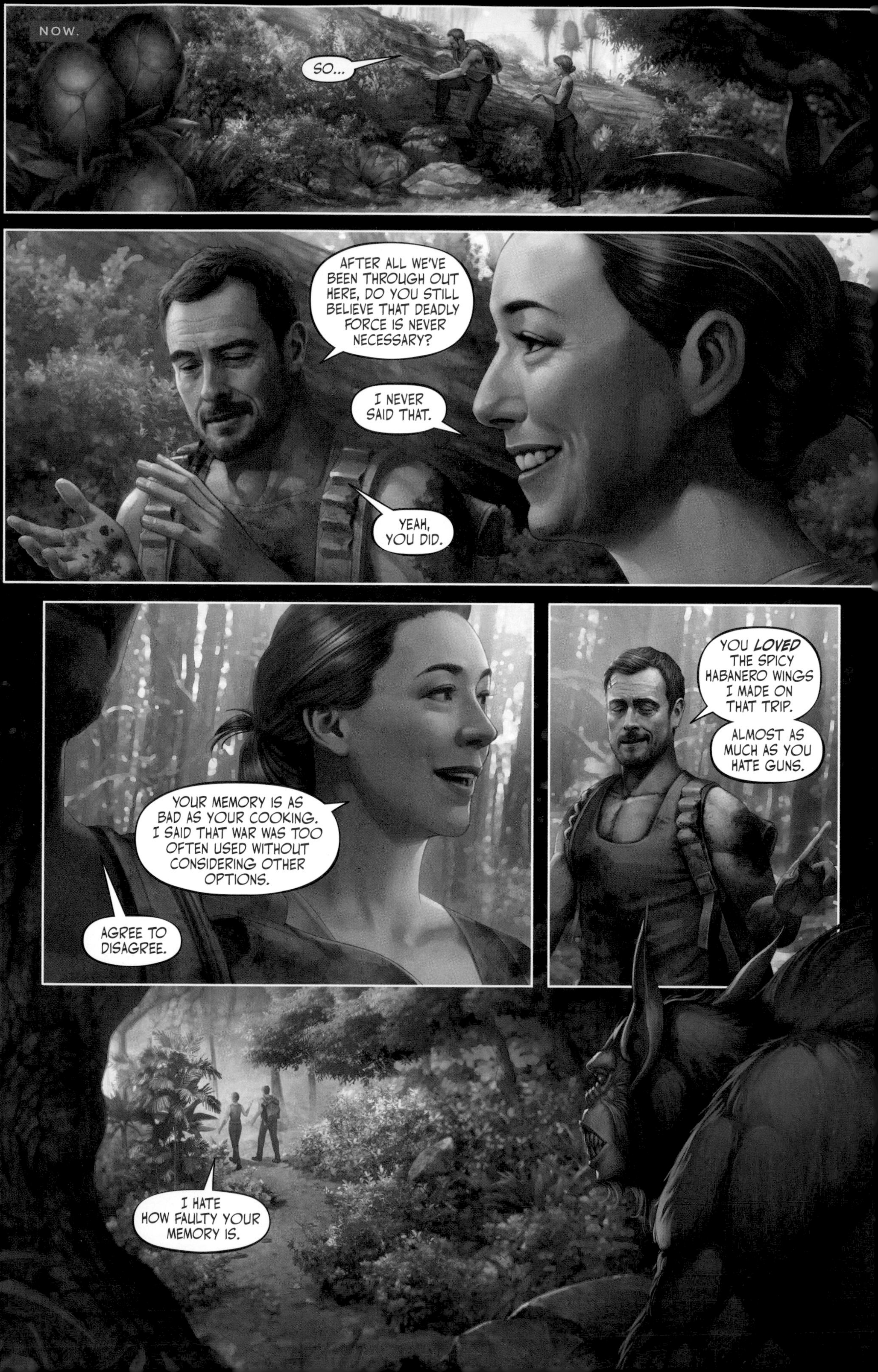
NOW.
SO...
AFTER ALL WE'VE BEEN THROUGH OUT HERE, DO YOU STILL BELIEVE THAT DEADLY FORCE IS NEVER NECESSARY?
I NEVER SAID THAT.
YEAH, YOU DID.
YOUR MEMORY IS AS BAD AS YOUR COOKING. I SAID THAT WAR WAS TOO OFTEN USED WITHOUT CONSIDERING OTHER OPTIONS.
AGREE TO DISAGREE.
YOU LOVED THE SPICY HABANERO WINGS I MADE ON THAT TRIP.
ALMOST AS MUCH AS YOU HATE GUNS.
I HATE HOW FAULTY YOUR MEMORY IS.

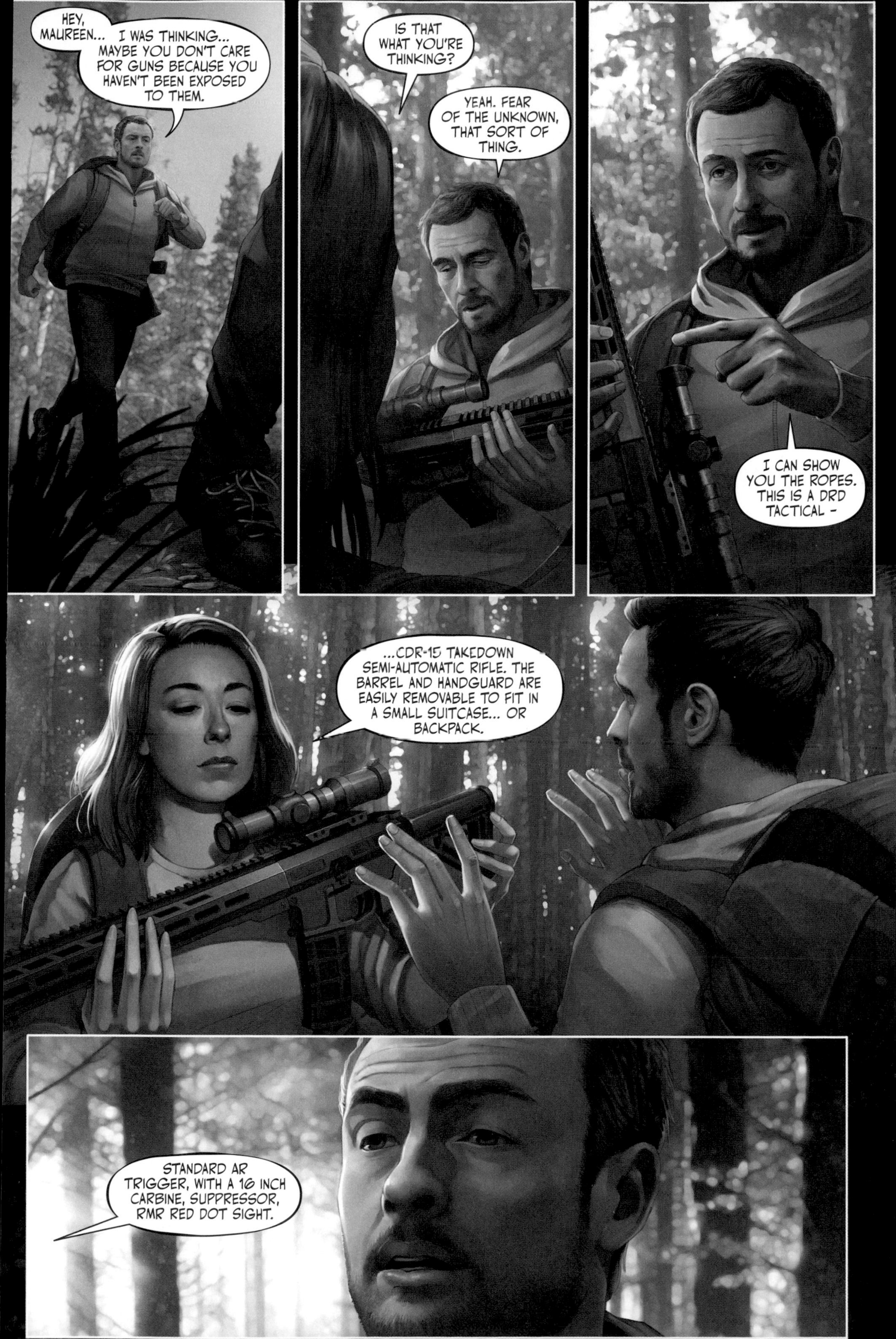
HEY, MAUREEN... I WAS THINKING... MAYBE YOU DON'T CARE FOR GUNS BECAUSE YOU HAVEN'T BEEN EXPOSED TO THEM.
IS THAT WHAT YOU'RE THINKING?
YEAH. FEAR OF THE UNKNOWN, THAT SORT OF THING.
I CAN SHOW YOU THE ROPES. THIS IS A DRD TACTICAL -
...CDR-15 TAKEDOWN SEMI-AUTOMATIC RIFLE. THE BARREL AND HANDGUARD ARE EASILY REMOVABLE TO FIT IN A SMALL SUITCASE... OR BACKPACK.
STANDARD AR TRIGGER, WITH A 16 INCH CARBINE, SUPPRESSOR, RMR RED DOT SIGHT.

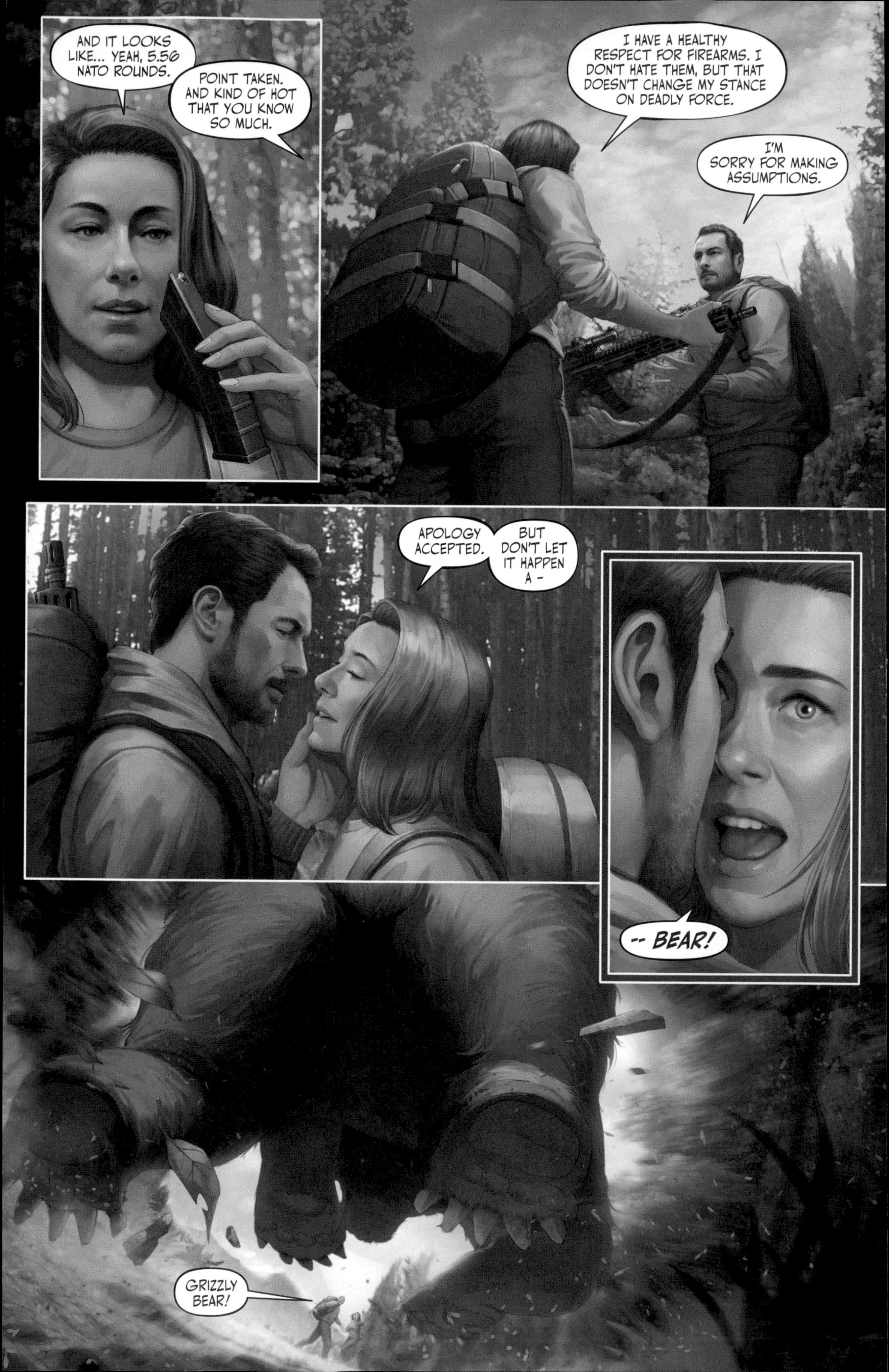
AND IT LOOKS LIKE... YEAH, 5.56 NATO ROUNDS.
POINT TAKEN. AND KIND OF HOT THAT YOU KNOW SO MUCH.
I HAVE A HEALTHY RESPECT FOR FIREARMS. I DON'T HATE THEM, BUT THAT DOESN'T CHANGE MY STANCE ON DEADLY FORCE.
I'M SORRY FOR MAKING ASSUMPTIONS.
APOLOGY ACCEPTED.
BUT DON'T LET IT HAPPEN A -
-- BEAR!
GRIZZLY BEAR!

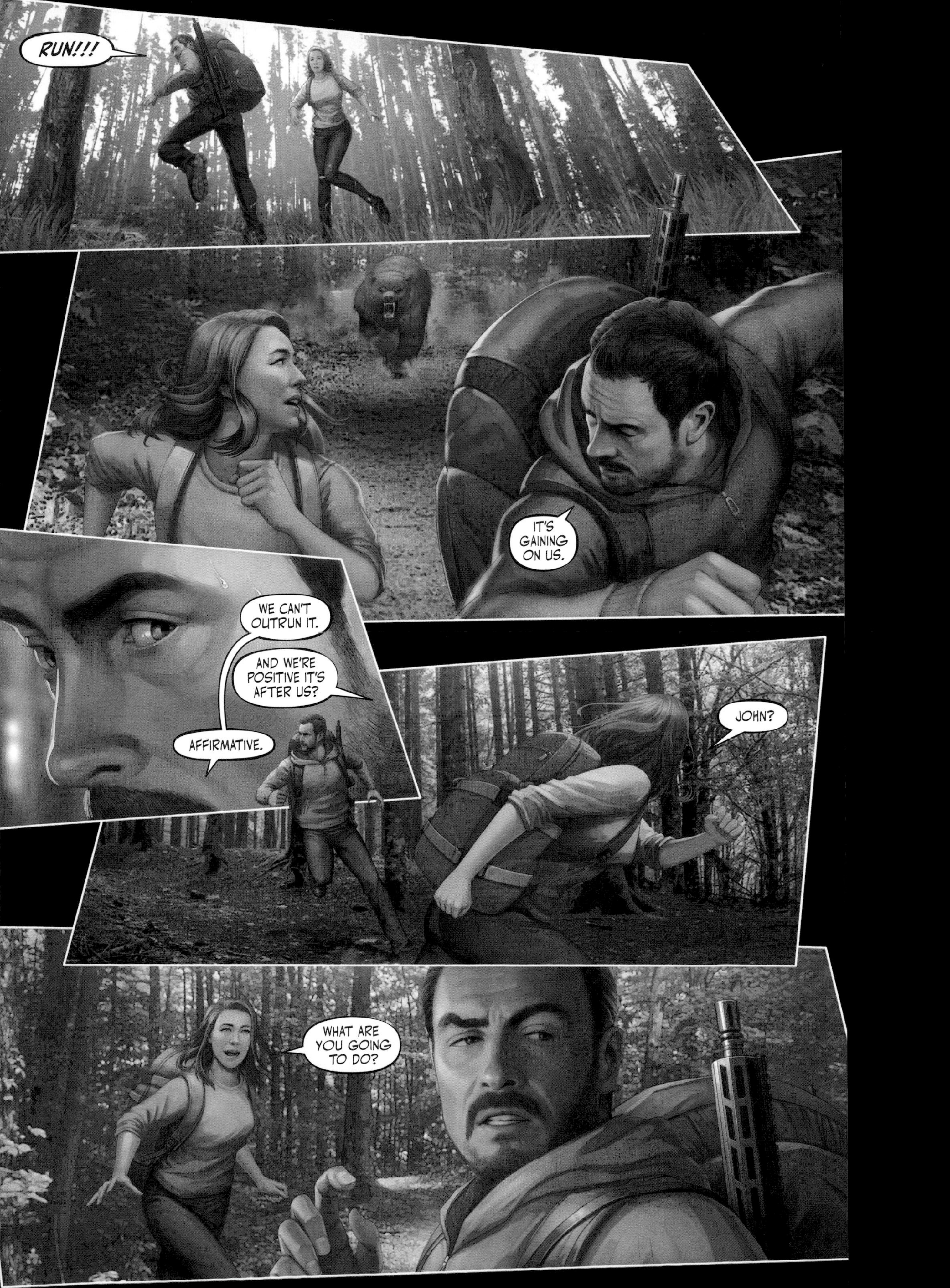
RUN!!!
IT'S GAINING ON US.
WE CAN'T OUTRUN IT.
AND WE'RE POSITIVE IT'S AFTER US?
AFFIRMATIVE.
JOHN?
WHAT ARE YOU GOING TO DO?

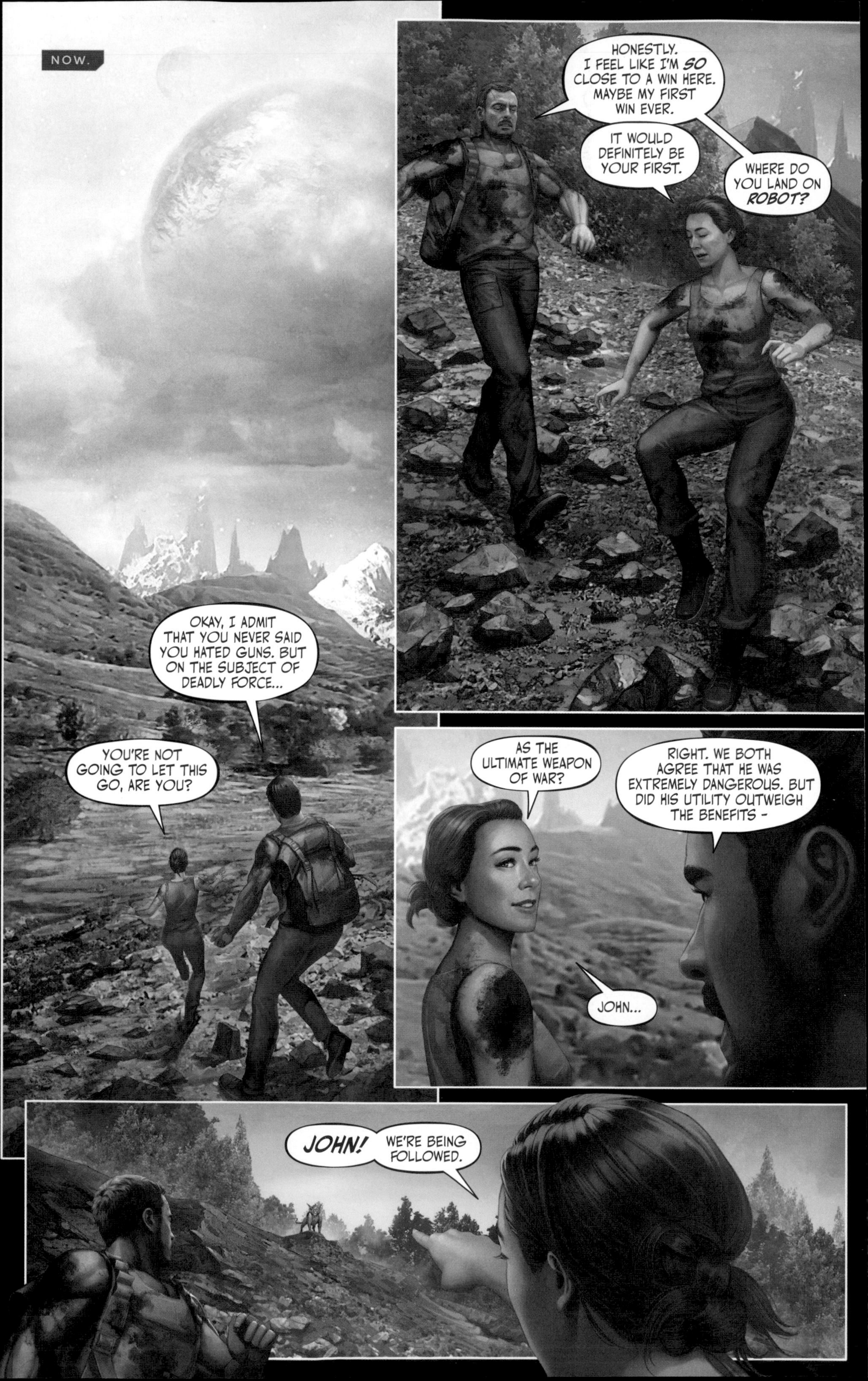
NOW.
OKAY, I ADMIT THAT YOU NEVER SAID YOU HATED GUNS. BUT ON THE SUBJECT OF DEADLY FORCE...
YOU'RE NOT GOING TO LET THIS GO, ARE YOU?
HONESTLY. I FEEL LIKE I'M SO CLOSE TO A WIN HERE. MAYBE MY FIRST WIN EVER.
IT WOULD DEFINITELY BE YOUR FIRST.
WHERE DO YOU LAND ON ROBOT?
AS THE ULTIMATE WEAPON OF WAR?
RIGHT. WE BOTH AGREE THAT HE WAS EXTREMELY DANGEROUS. BUT DID HIS UTILITY OUTWEIGH THE BENEFITS -
JOHN...
JOHN!
WE'RE BEING FOLLOWED.

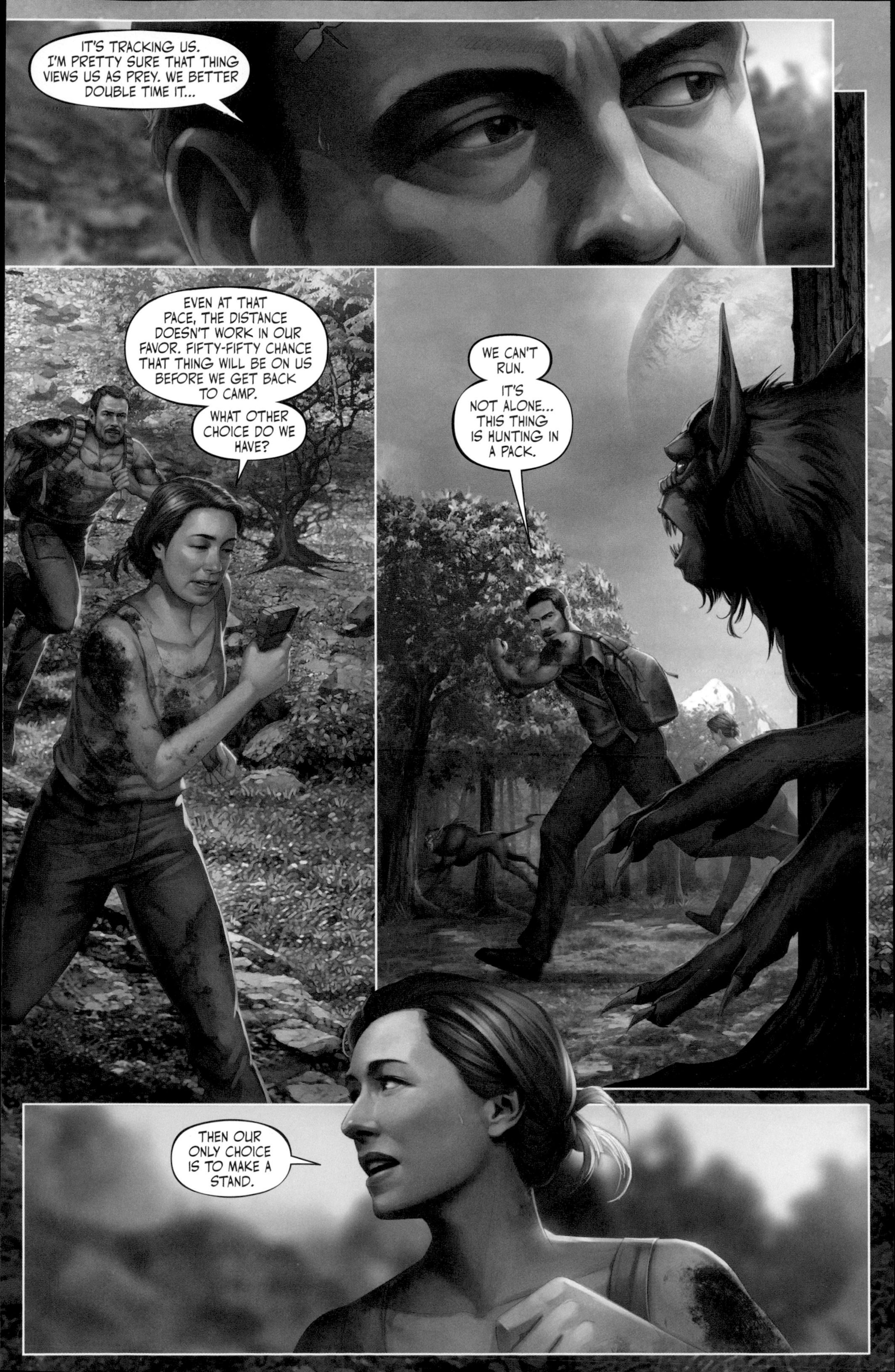
IT'S TRACKING US. I'M PRETTY SURE THAT THING VIEWS US AS PREY. WE BETTER DOUBLE TIME IT...
EVEN AT THAT PACE, THE DISTANCE DOESN'T WORK IN OUR FAVOR. FIFTY-FIFTY CHANCE THAT THING WILL BE ON US BEFORE WE GET BACK TO CAMP.
WHAT OTHER CHOICE DO WE HAVE?
WE CAN'T RUN.
IT'S NOT ALONE... THIS THING IS HUNTING IN A PACK.
THEN OUR ONLY CHOICE IS TO MAKE A STAND.

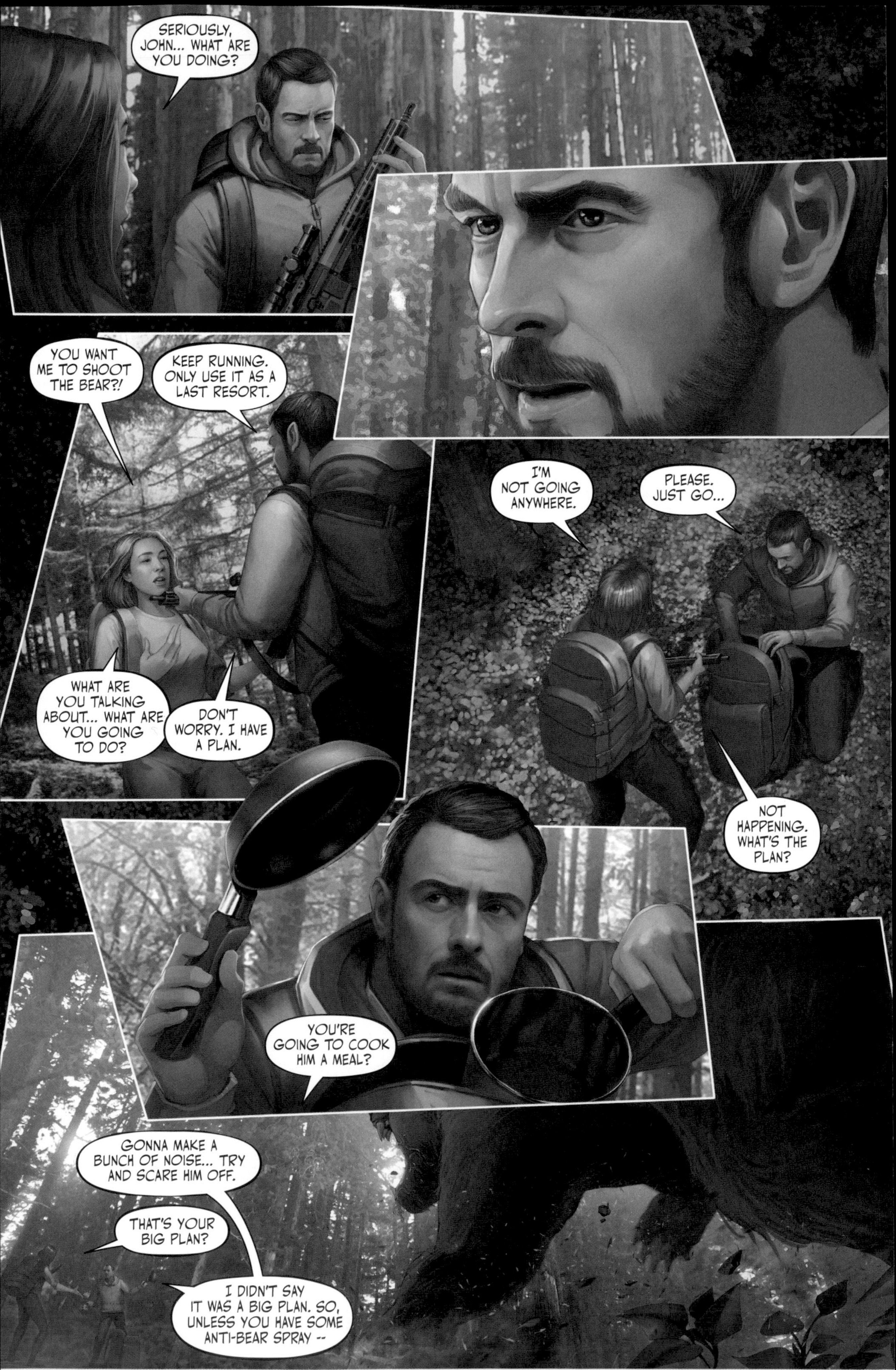
SERIOUSLY, JOHN... WHAT ARE YOU DOING?
YOU WANT ME TO SHOOT THE BEAR?!
KEEP RUNNING. ONLY USE IT AS A LAST RESORT.
WHAT ARE YOU TALKING ABOUT... WHAT ARE YOU GOING TO DO?
DON'T WORRY. I HAVE A PLAN.
I'M NOT GOING ANYWHERE.
PLEASE. JUST GO...
NOT HAPPENING. WHAT'S THE PLAN?
YOU'RE GOING TO COOK HIM A MEAL?
GONNA MAKE A BUNCH OF NOISE... TRY AND SCARE HIM OFF.
THAT'S YOUR BIG PLAN?
I DIDN'T SAY IT WAS A BIG PLAN. SO, UNLESS YOU HAVE SOME ANTI-BEAR SPRAY --

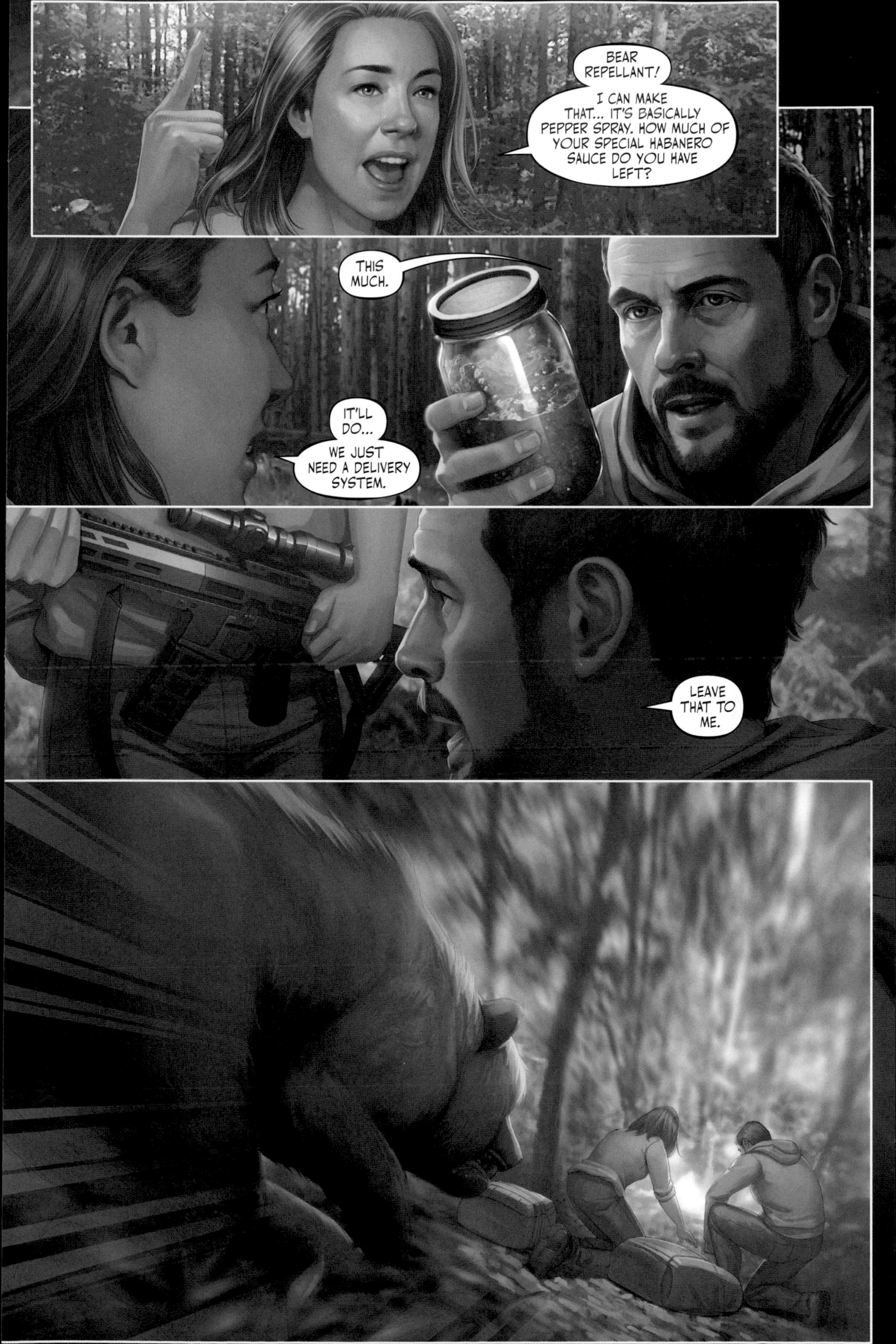
BEAR REPELLANT!
I CAN MAKE THAT... IT'S BASICALLY PEPPER SPRAY. HOW MUCH OF YOUR SPECIAL HABANERO SAUCE DO YOU HAVE LEFT?
THIS MUCH.
IT'LL DO...
WE JUST NEED A DELIVERY SYSTEM.
LEAVE THAT TO ME.

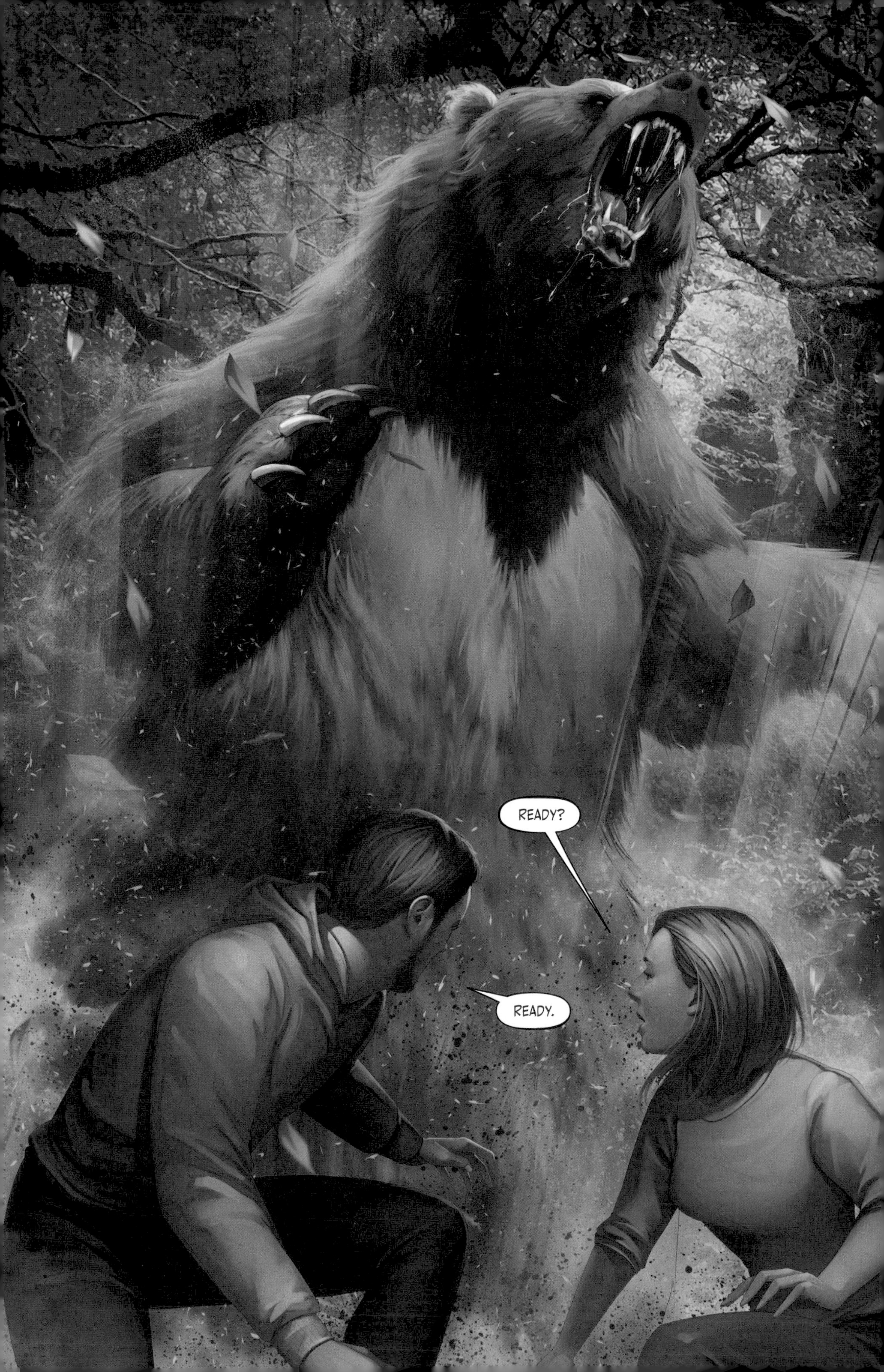
READY?
READY.

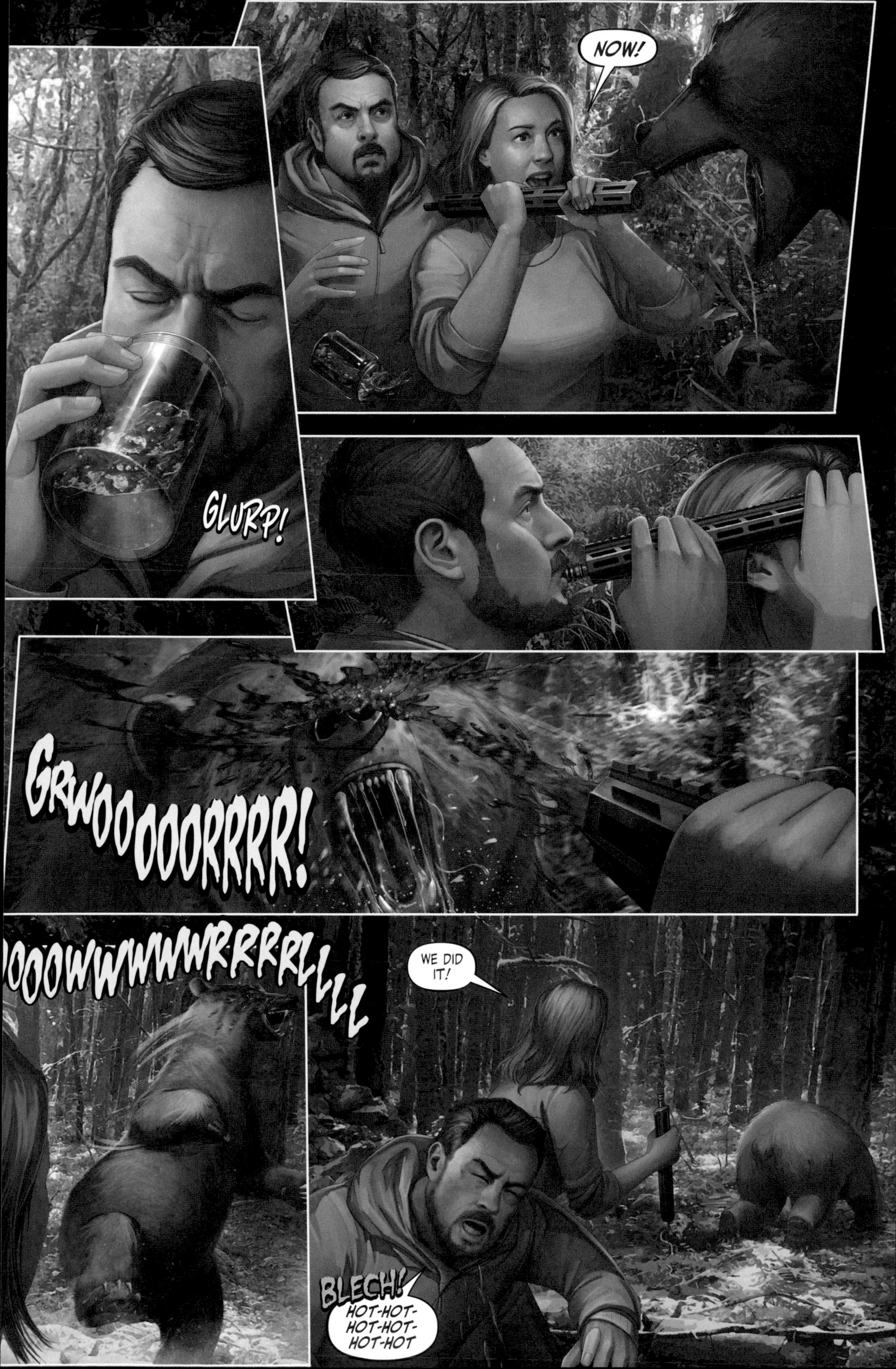
NOW!
GLURP!
GRWOOOOORRRR!
OOOOWWWWRRRRLLLL
WE DID IT!
BLECH!
HOT-HOT-HOT-HOT-HOT-HOT

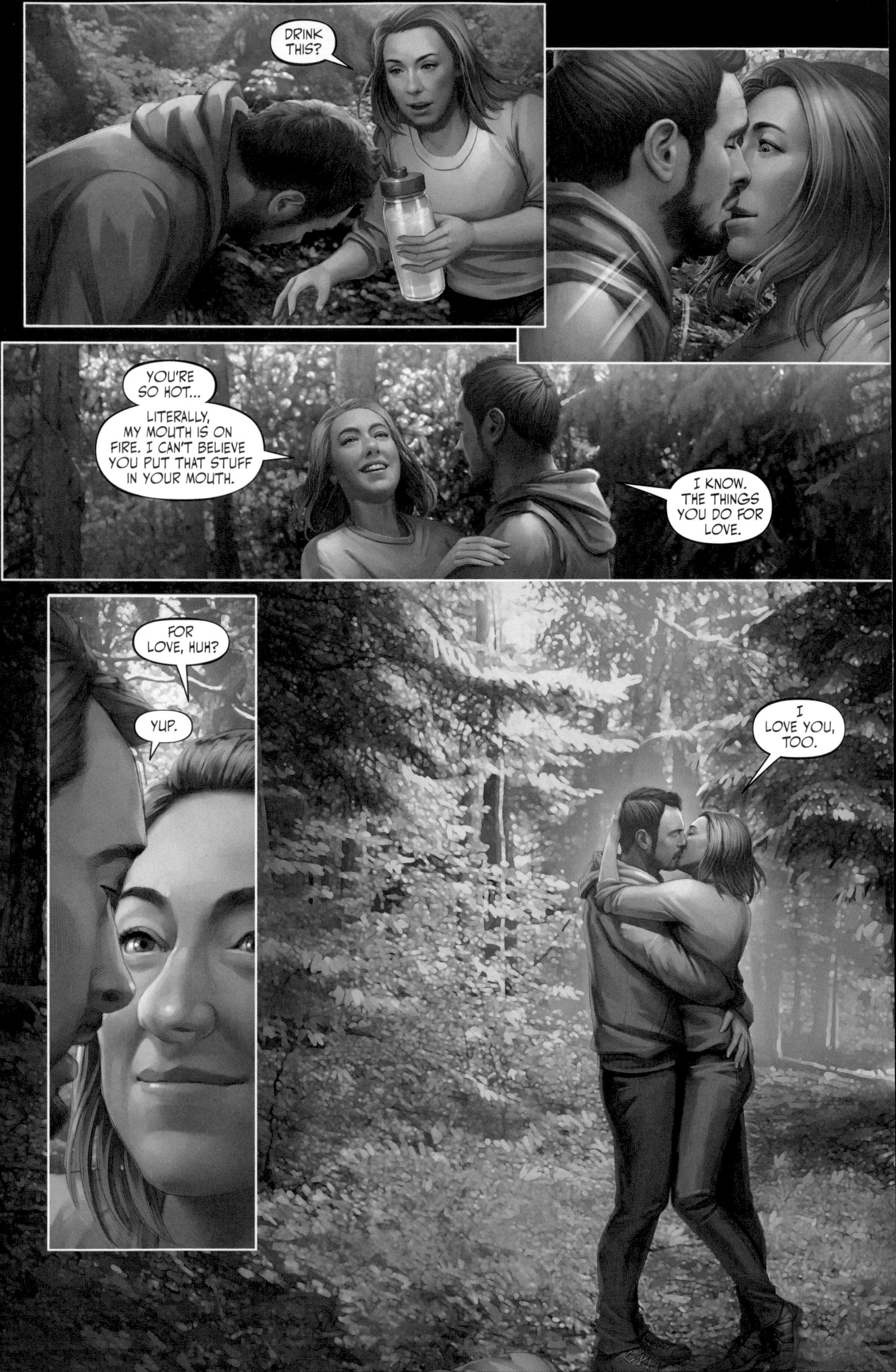
DRINK THIS?
YOU'RE SO HOT...
LITERALLY, MY MOUTH IS ON FIRE. I CAN'T BELIEVE YOU PUT THAT STUFF IN YOUR MOUTH.
I KNOW. THE THINGS YOU DO FOR LOVE.
FOR LOVE, HUH?
YUP.
I LOVE YOU, TOO.

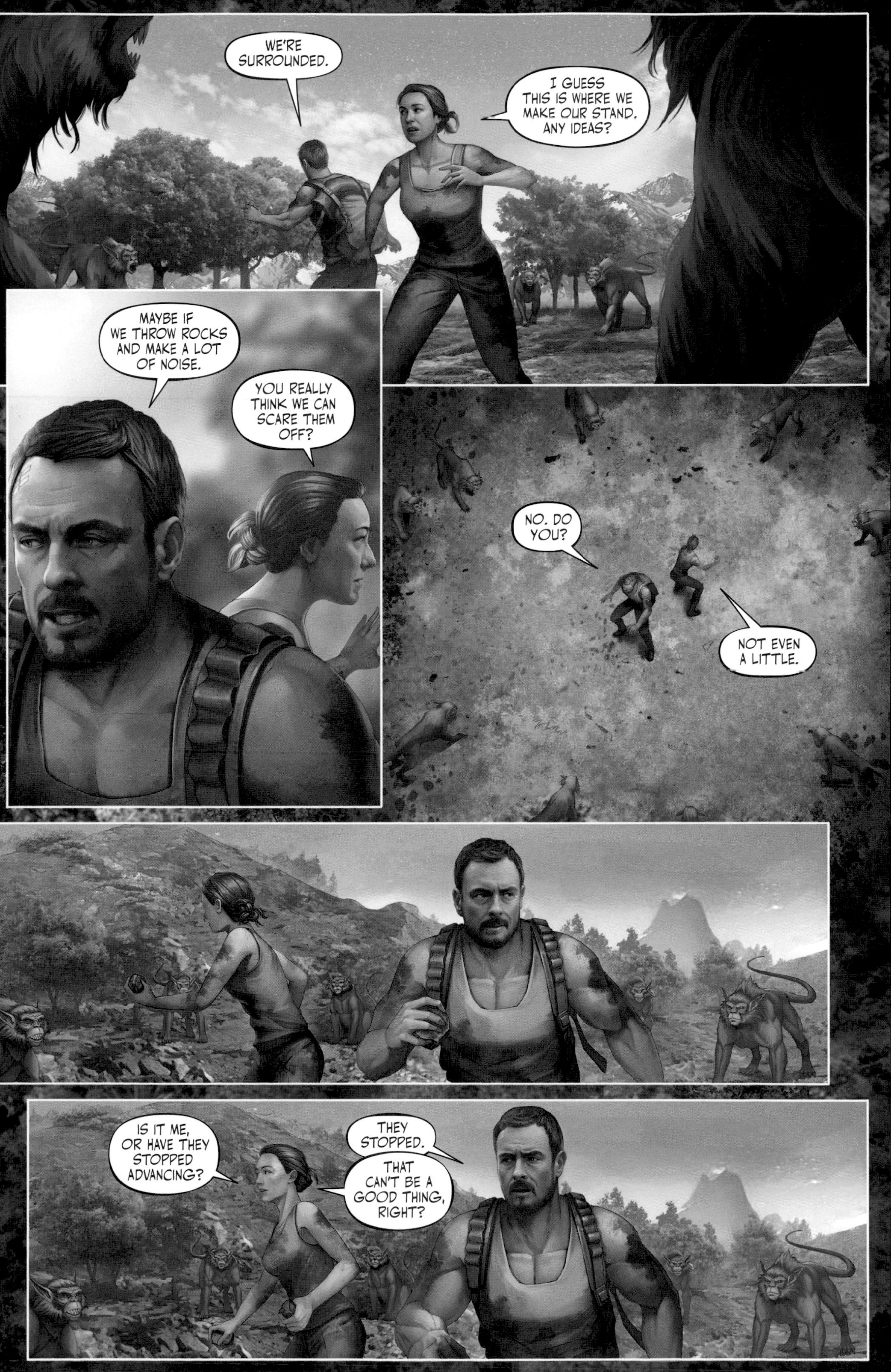
WE'RE SURROUNDED.
I GUESS THIS IS WHERE WE MAKE OUR STAND. ANY IDEAS?
MAYBE IF WE THROW ROCKS AND MAKE A LOT OF NOISE.
YOU REALLY THINK WE CAN SCARE THEM OFF?
NO. DO YOU?
NOT EVEN A LITTLE.
IS IT ME, OR HAVE THEY STOPPED ADVANCING?
THEY STOPPED.
THAT CAN'T BE A GOOD THING, RIGHT?

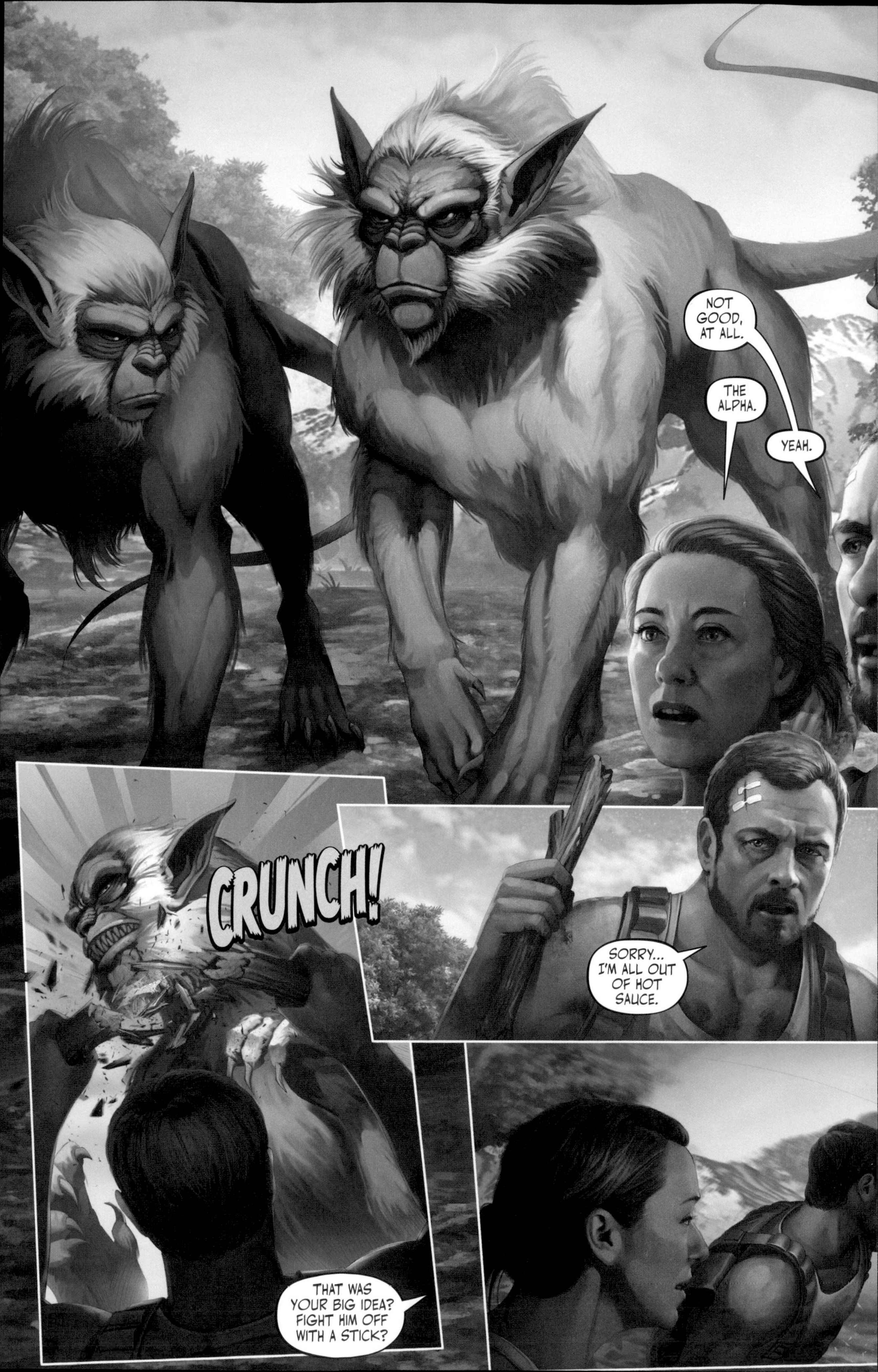
NOT GOOD, AT ALL.
THE ALPHA.
YEAH.
CRUNCH!
SORRY... I'M ALL OUT OF HOT SAUCE.
THAT WAS YOUR BIG IDEA? FIGHT HIM OFF WITH A STICK?

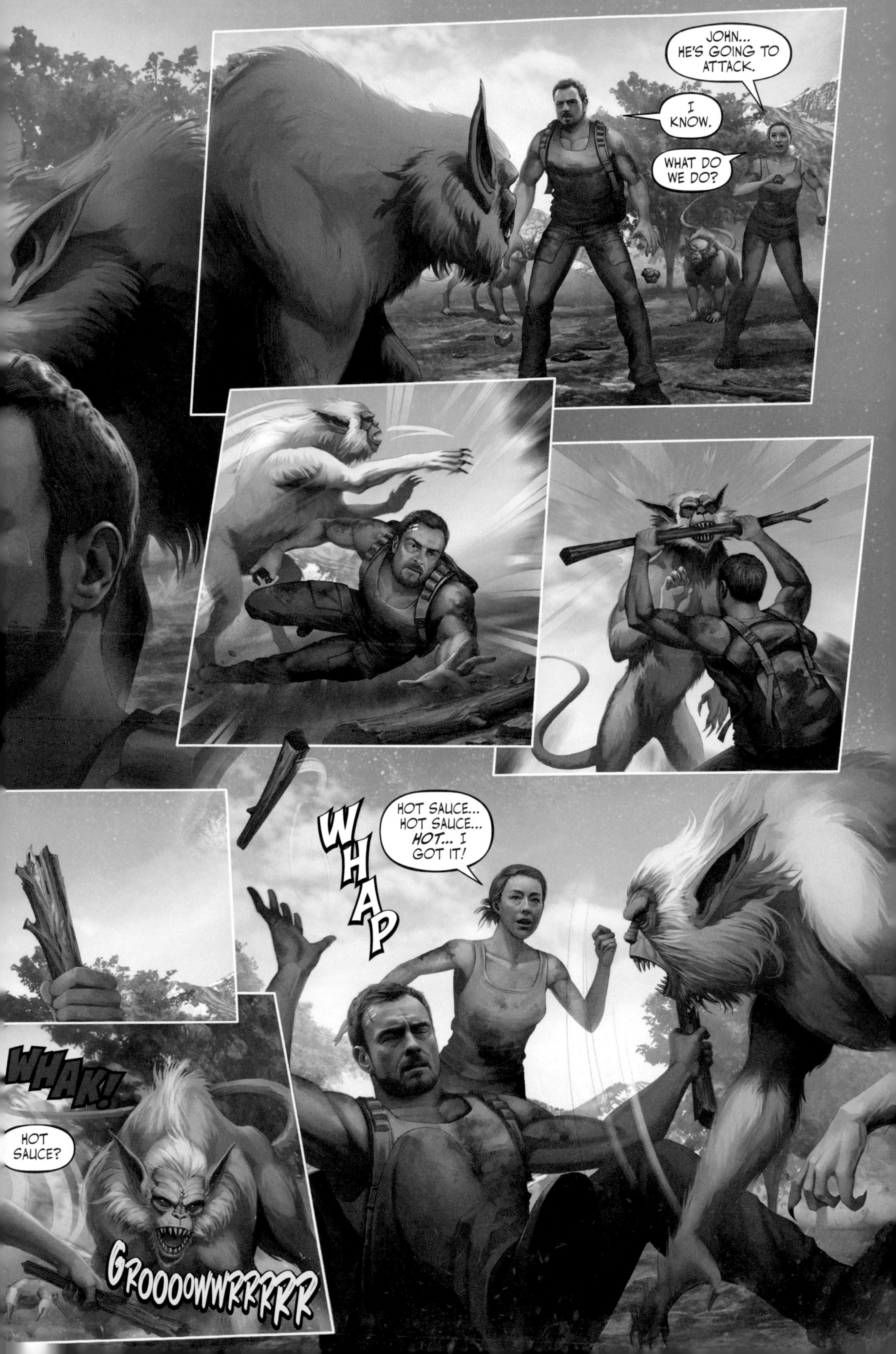
JOHN... HE'S GOING TO ATTACK.
I KNOW.
WHAT DO WE DO?
WHAP
HOT SAUCE... HOT SAUCE... HOT... I GOT IT!
WHAK!
HOT SAUCE?
GROOOOWWRRRRR

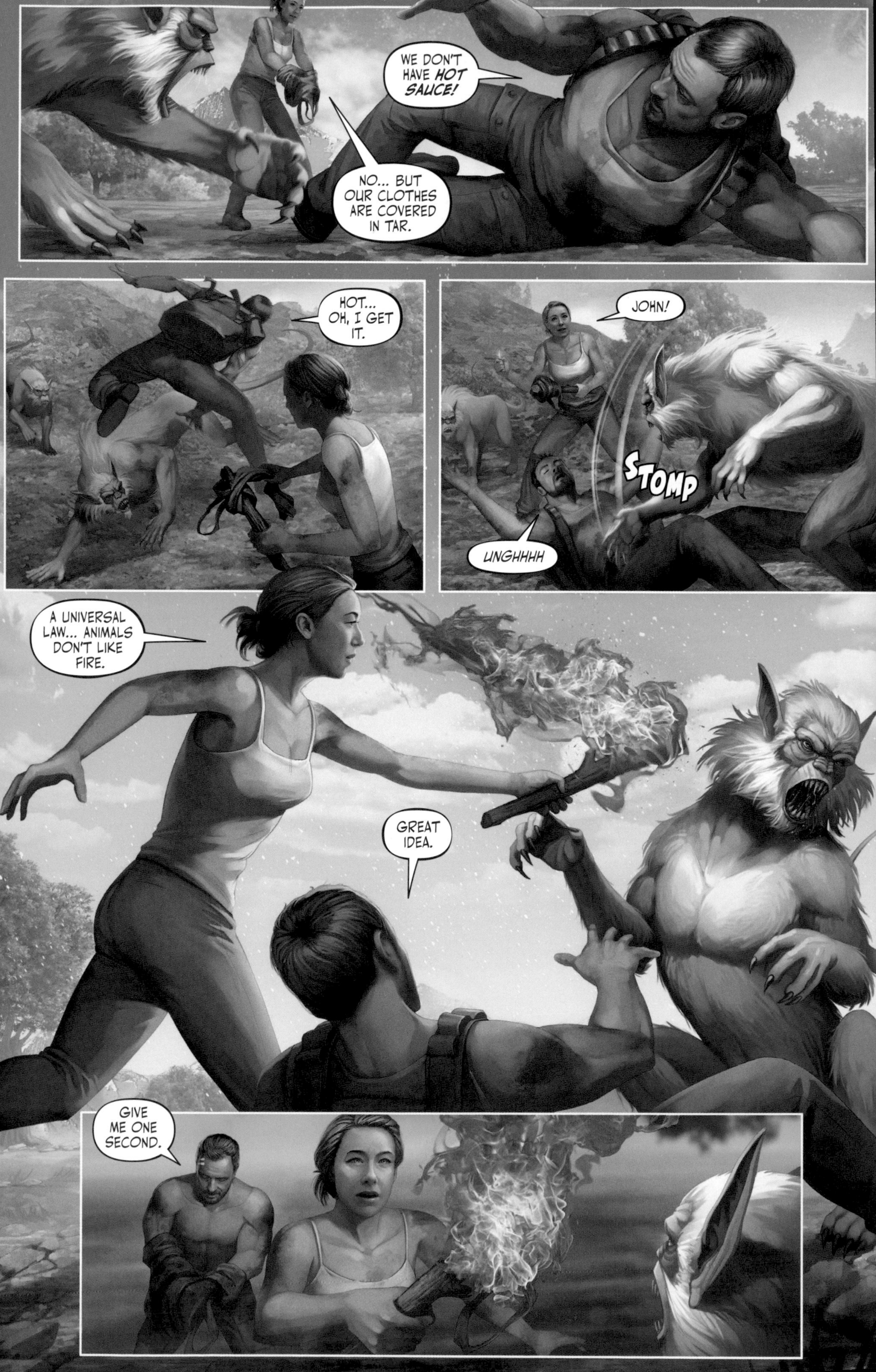
WE DON'T HAVE HOT SAUCE!
NO... BUT OUR CLOTHES ARE COVERED IN TAR.
HOT... OH, I GET IT.
JOHN!
STOMP
UNGHHHH
A UNIVERSAL LAW... ANIMALS DON'T LIKE FIRE.
GREAT IDEA.
GIVE ME ONE SECOND.

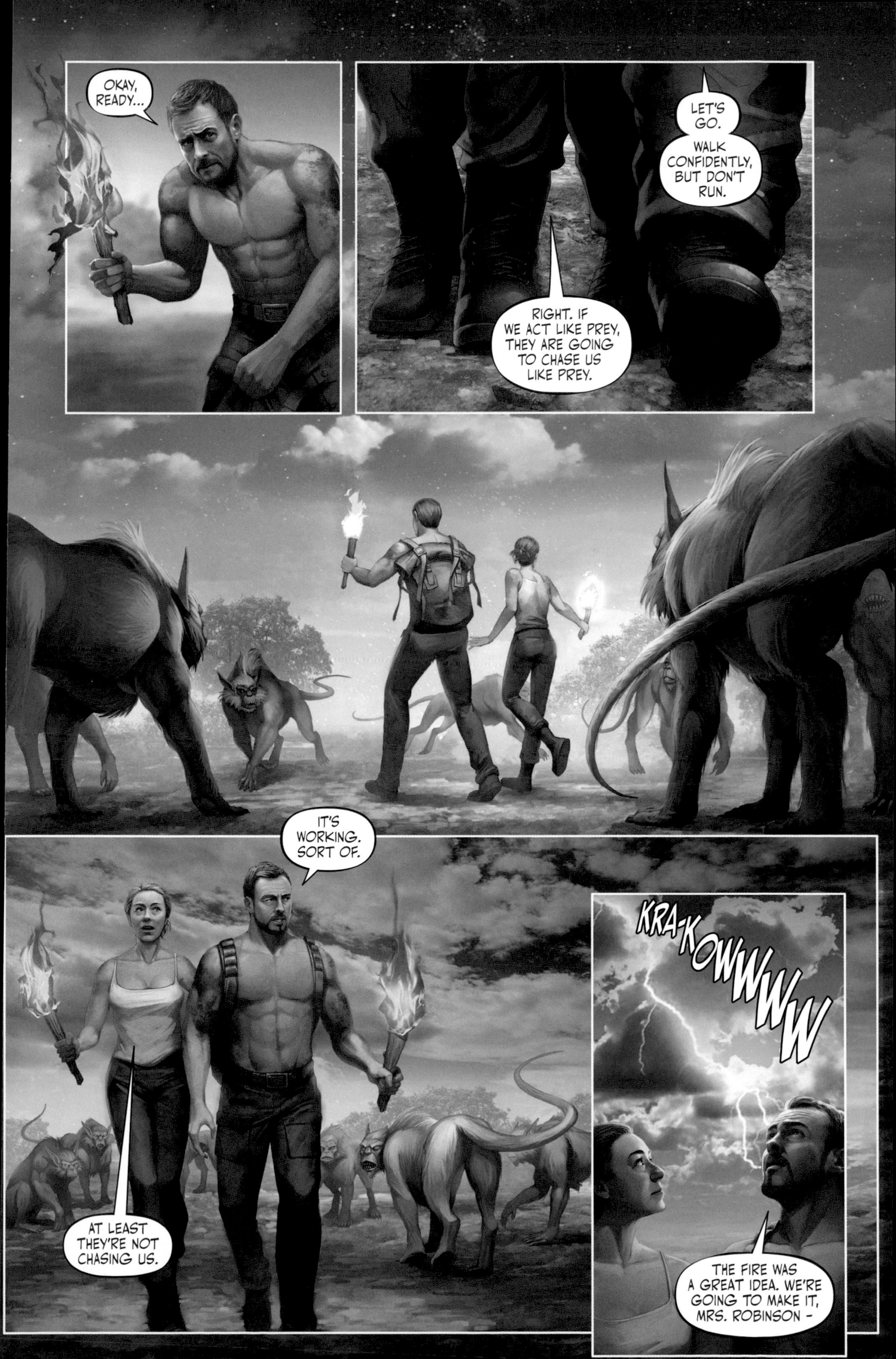
OKAY, READY...
LET'S GO.
WALK CONFIDENTLY, BUT DON'T RUN.
RIGHT. IF WE ACT LIKE PREY, THEY ARE GOING TO CHASE US LIKE PREY.
IT'S WORKING. SORT OF.
AT LEAST THEY'RE NOT CHASING US.
KRA-KOWWWWW
THE FIRE WAS A GREAT IDEA. WE'RE GOING TO MAKE IT, MRS. ROBINSON -

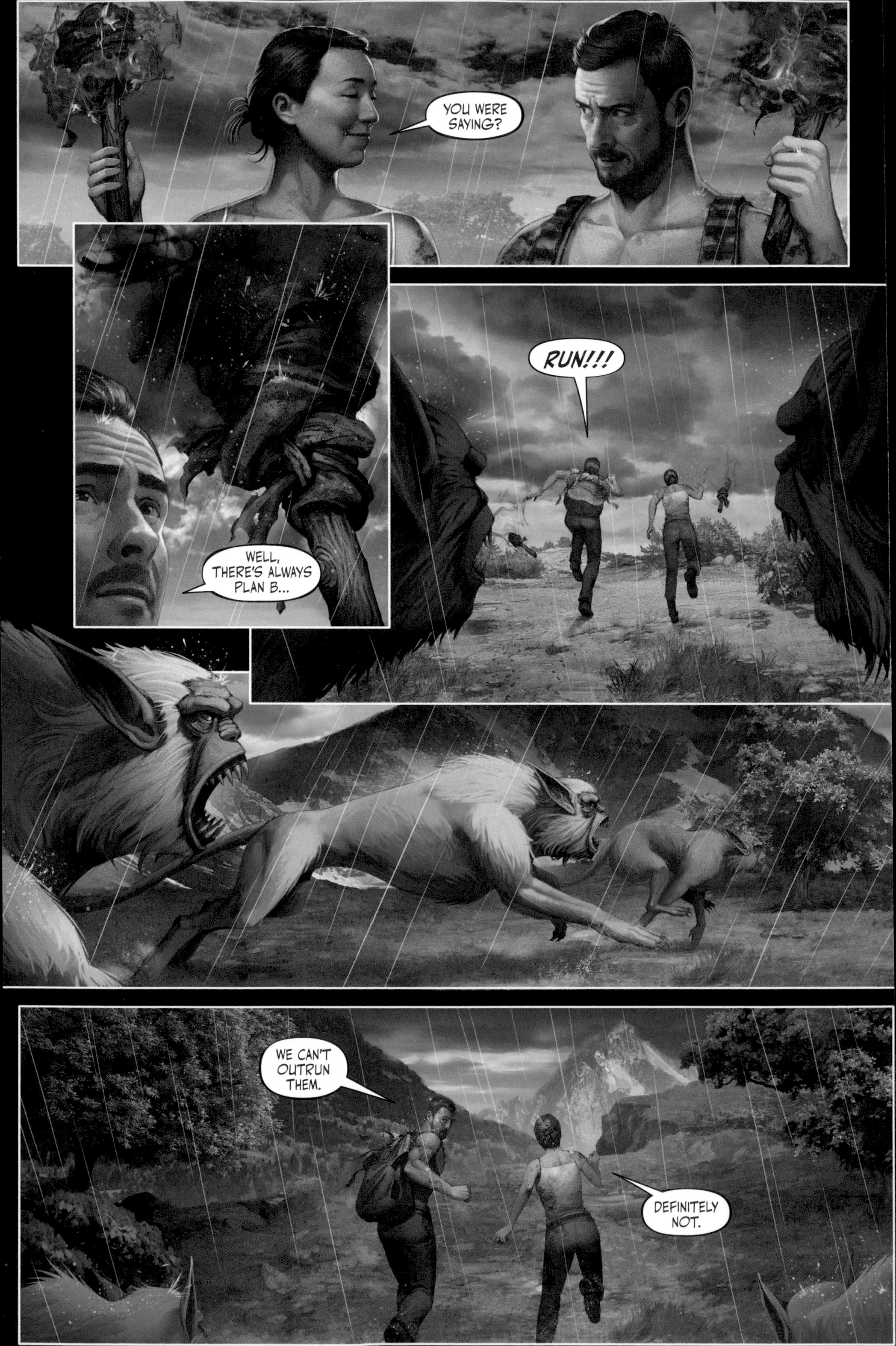
YOU WERE SAYING?
WELL, THERE'S ALWAYS PLAN B...
RUN!!!
WE CAN'T OUTRUN THEM.
DEFINITELY NOT.

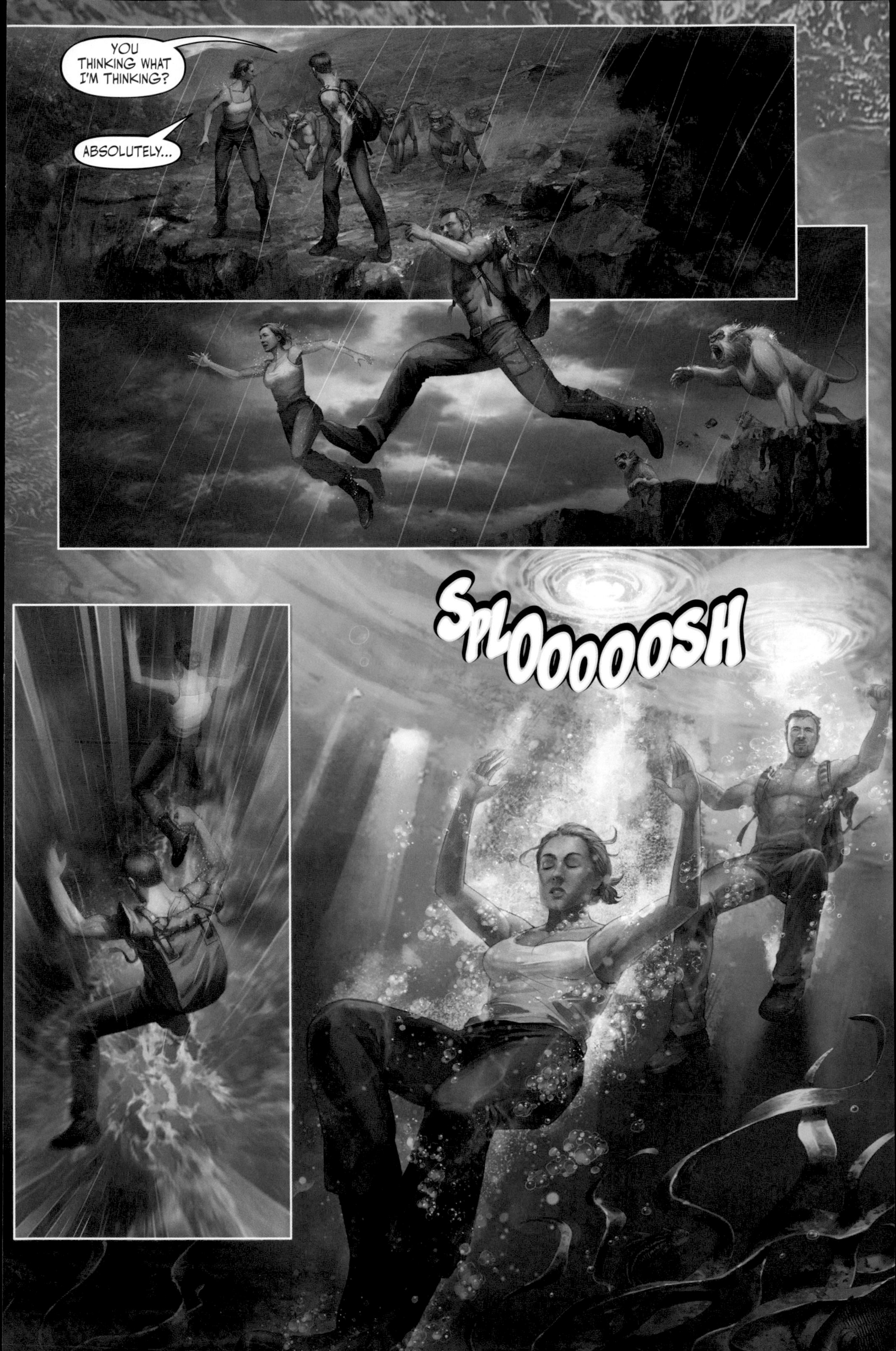
YOU THINKING WHAT I'M THINKING?
ABSOLUTELY...
SPLOOOOOOSH

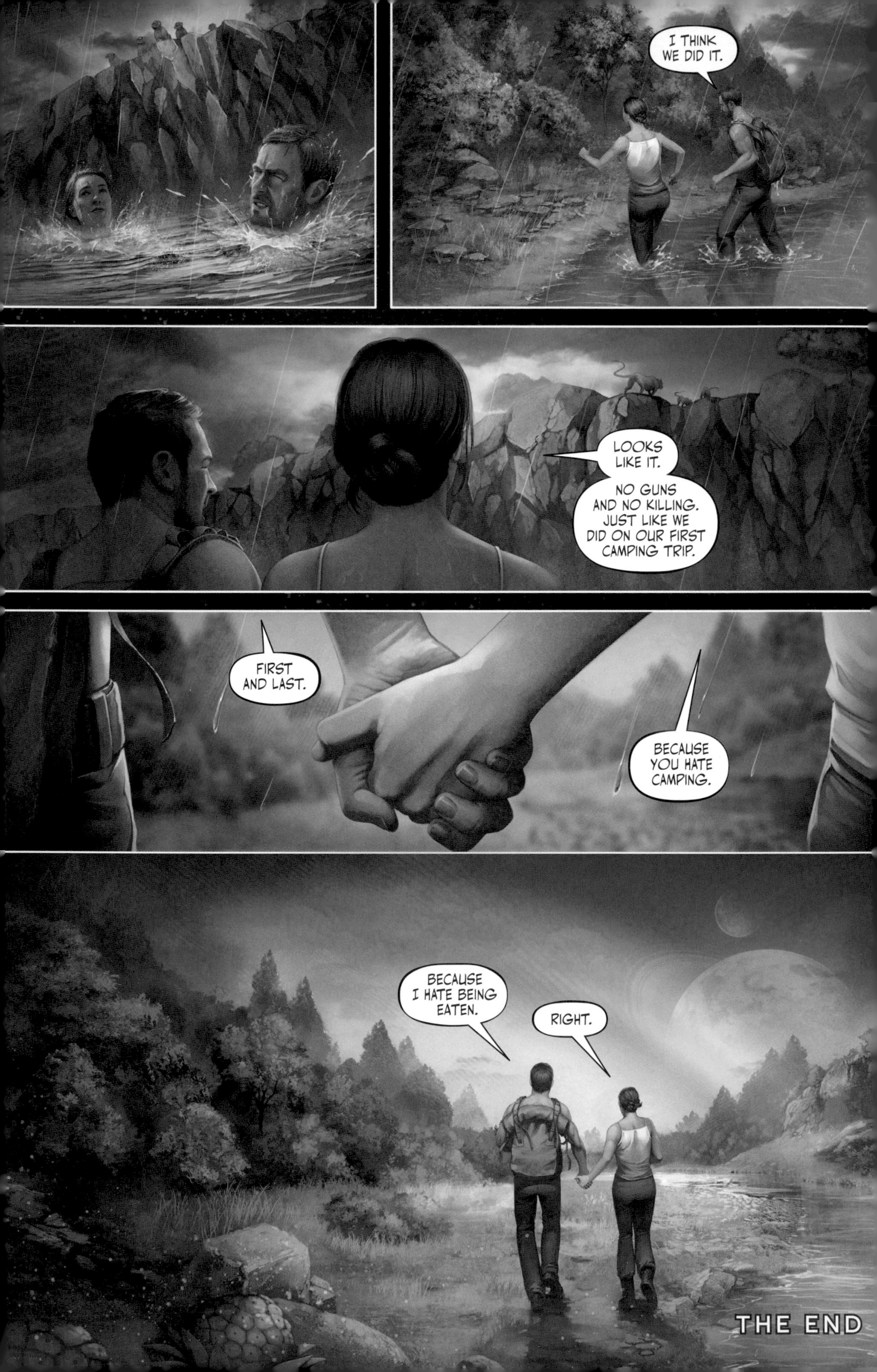
I THINK WE DID IT.
LOOKS LIKE IT.
NO GUNS AND NO KILLING. JUST LIKE WE DID ON OUR FIRST CAMPING TRIP.
FIRST AND LAST.
BECAUSE YOU HATE CAMPING.
BECAUSE I HATE BEING EATEN.
RIGHT.
THE END

PREVIEW OF
NEXT VOLUME:

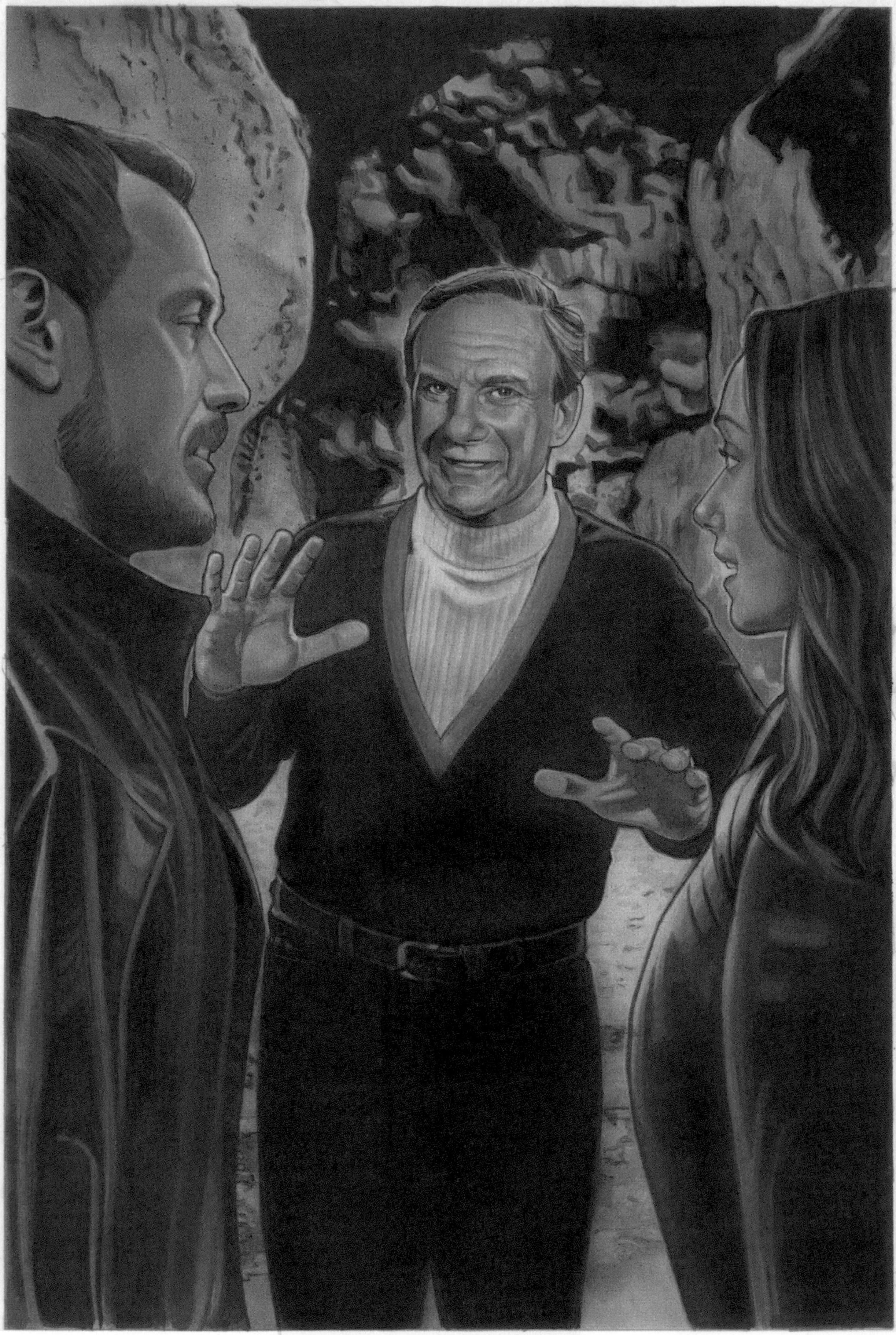

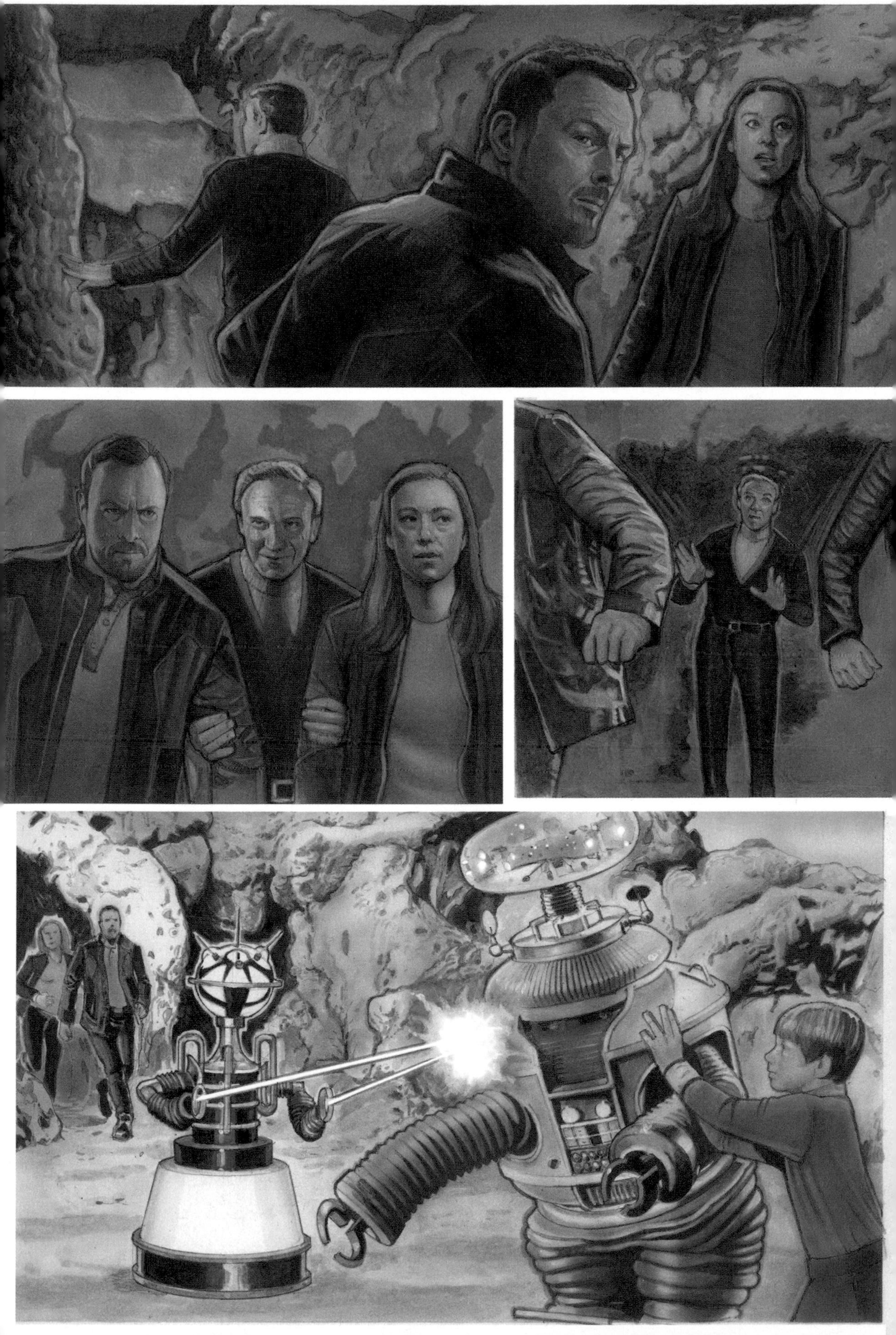

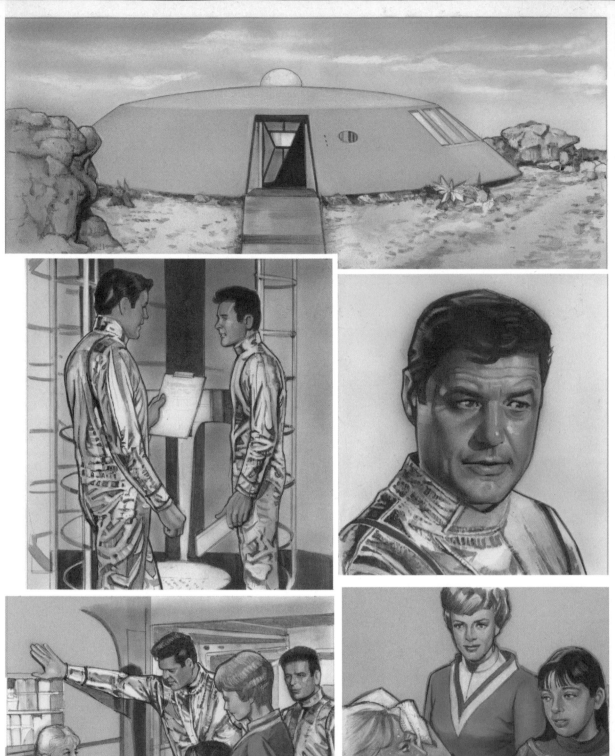

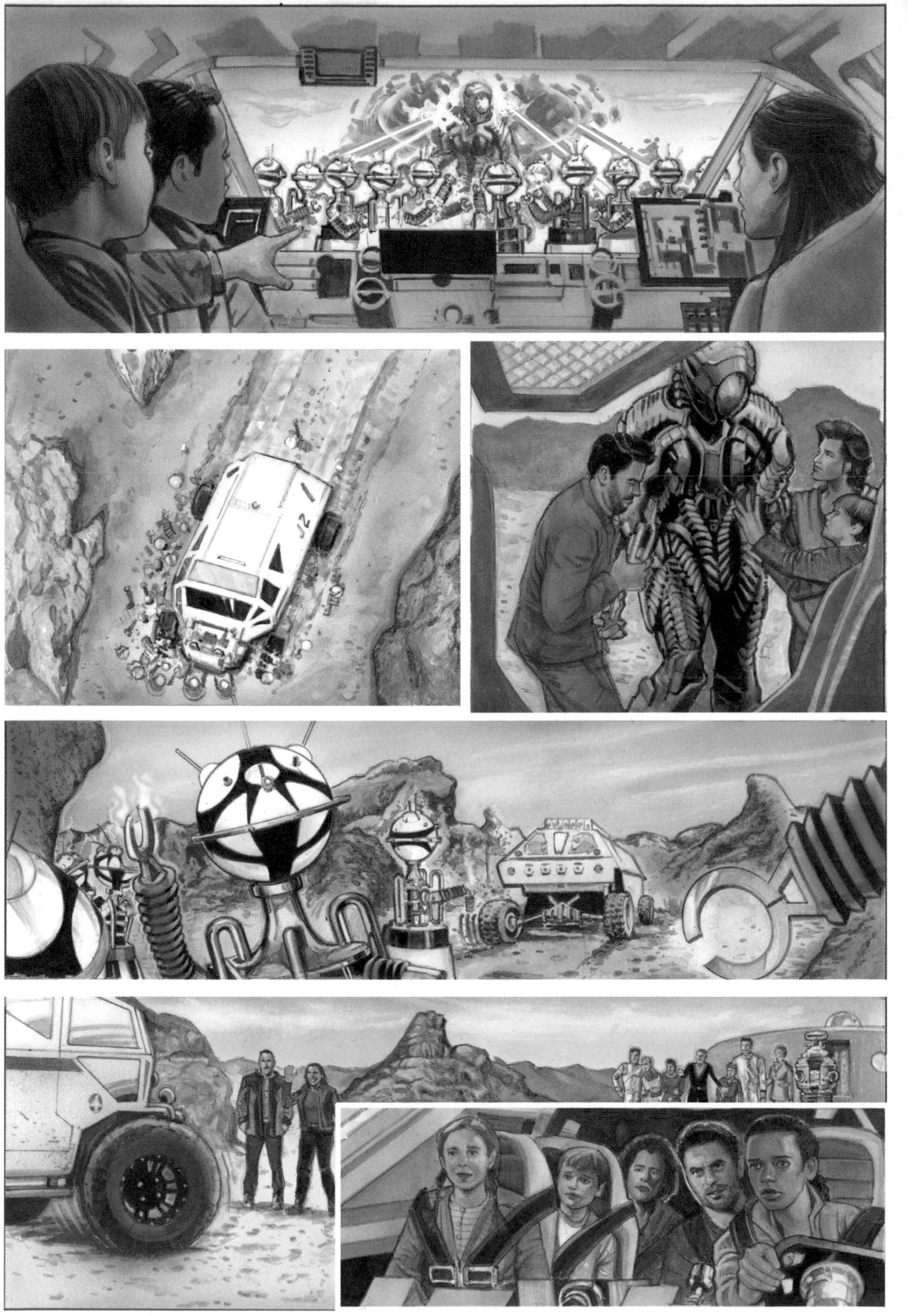

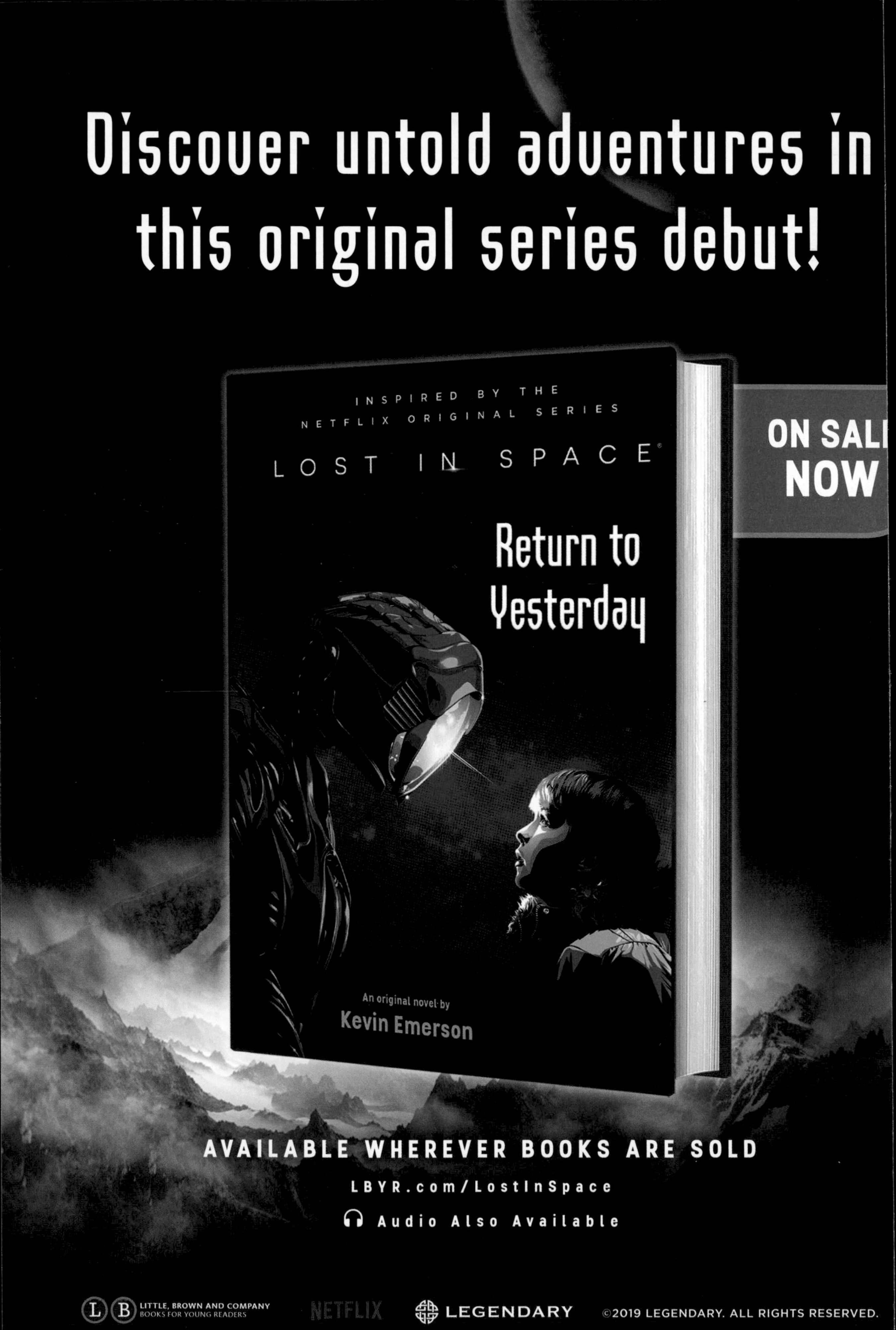
Discover untold adventures in this original series debut!
INSPIRED BY THE NETFLIX ORIGINAL SERIES
LOST IN SPACE®
Return to Yesterday
An original novel by
Kevin Emerson
ON SAL
NOW
AVAILABLE WHEREVER BOOKS ARE SOLD
LBYR.com/LostInSpace
Audio Also Available
LITTLE, BROWN AND COMPANY
BOOKS FOR YOUNG READERS
NETFLIX
LEGENDARY
©2019 LEGENDARY. ALL RIGHTS RESERVED.